*Twayne's English Authors Series*

Sylvia E. Bowman, *Editor*

INDIANA UNIVERSITY

*John Davidson*

(TEAS) 143

# JOHN DAVIDSON

*By* CARROLL V. PETERSON

*Fort Lewis College*

Twayne Publishers, Inc. :: New York

# *Preface*

In these times of chronic value crises and endemic conflicts between the humane and the technological, the study of the roots of our problems seems to afford us a rational method of clarifying the issues. We surely do not need to be told again that the conflicts of the later twentieth century got their start in the technological revolution of the nineteenth, but we may perhaps still need an occasional reminder that it is not fair to blame the nineteenth century for our predicament; for the nineteenth century saw the issues and argued over them vigorously and honestly, sometimes resolving them and sometimes not.

John Davidson (1857–1909) is one of those nineteenth-century men who was extraordinarily aware of the trends of his times. At times he conformed to the trends; at other times he differed forcefully. But he reflects the intellectual and literary history of the period from about 1880 to 1909 in an unusual way. Thus, I believe it is worthwhile to take another look at Davidson's responses to materialism, to hero worship, and to imperialism because his work so neatly illustrates for us the roots of our problems.

In keeping with the intent of the Twayne English Authors Series, this is a critical and analytical study of the writings of John Davidson: poetry, drama, prose fiction, nonfictional prose, criticism, and personal correspondence. For the first time, therefore, all of the genres in which Davidson wrote have been brought to bear on a study of the growth of his mind. This book is based on my extensive examination of all of Davidson's known writings, including his hundreds of publications in newspapers and periodicals, and the correspondence which has been collected, as well as the published books.

My organization is historical, partly because I believe that liberal and humane learning is always historical, but also because the thesis of this book is that we can trace the growth of the writer's mind by analyzing what he wrote. However, the book is not biography: only where some biographical fact is relevent to the writings themselves is biography emphasized. Each of the major publications—plays, novels, long poems—has received individual attention, with the exception of a few obviously light-weight pieces, such as *Laura Ruthven's Widowhood, Baptist Lake,* and *An Unhistorical Pastoral.* The volumes of shorter poems are represented by writings typical both of stylistic and ideological development. Short stories, criticism, nonfictional prose, and letters have been selected to support and explain the development evidenced in the major publications, as well as in the representative poems.

When it is relevant to Davidson's development, I have cited his relationship to his contemporaries as well as to predecessors who seem to have influenced him. Since there is not enough space in a book of this length to trace all the possible influences, I have concentrated on the central lines of influence—the major English Romantic poets, Carlyle, Swinburne, Nietzsche, and British imperialism.

I am indebted to many people. Professor Frederick McDowell of the University of Iowa has been a generous and humane advisor since graduate school days. Professor J. Benjamin Townsend of the State University of New York at Buffalo allowed me to use his large file of copies of Davidson's correspondence. He has continued to assist me in many ways, not the least of which was to encourage me to go ahead with my work by suggesting that even though he seemed to have been over the same ground already, there was still something to be done. The librarians at the University of Iowa, the State University of New York at Buffalo, the University of Illinois, and Illinois State University have, in their quiet and unspectacular way, assisted me more than they know. My special appreciation goes to Yale University Press for permission to quote extensively from Professor Townsend's *John Davidson: Poet of Armageddon.* Last but not least, a word to Maxine, who has, in all sorts of ways, helped me to write this book.

C.V.P.

*Fort Lewis College*
*December, 1971*

# Contents

# Contents

# *Chronology*

This chronology is not an exhaustive list of important events in Davidson's life; rather, I have included those things which may have affected the development of his ideas. Some of the items will help to show why I have divided his career into three periods, and a few items are there purely for their biographical interest. The source for most of the information in the chronology is J. Benjamin Townsend's *John Davidson: Poet of Armageddon.*

1857    John Davidson born April 11 at Barrhead, Renfrewshire, in southwestern Scotland, about six miles south of Glasgow; son of Alexander and Helen Davidson: one of three children.

c. 1859    Family moved to Glasgow, where Davidson's father had been appointed pastor of the Evangelical Union Church in Montrose Street.

c. 1861    Family moved to Greenock where Davidson attended Highlander's Academy.

1869    Wrote his first poem, "a sturdy ballad on the defeat of the Moors by Pamiro king of Spain."

1870    Left school to work in the chemical laboratory of Walker's, a Greenock company.

1871    With passage of Food Adulteration Act, became assistant to the Public Analyst in Greenock.

1872–    Pupil-teacher at Highlander's Academy. Much read-
1876    ing of English literature and European literature in translation.

1876    Left Greenock to attend Edinburgh University for one session. No record of courses taken or books read.

1877    Wrote first play, *An Unhistorical Pastoral.*

| | |
|---|---|
| 1877–1878 | Taught at "Alexander's Charity," or Alexander's Endowed School. Became acquainted with John Nichol, a professor of English at Glasgow University. Nichol a friend of Alexander Smith, Sidney Dobell, and Algernon Swinburne, whom Davidson met at Nichol's home in 1878. |
| 1878–1881 | English master at Perth Academy; perhaps met his future wife. Dismissed for conduct unbecoming an English master—that is, reciting such set pieces as "Tam o'Shanter" at local concerts and entertainments. |
| 1881–1882 | Taught at Kelvinside Academy in Glasgow. |
| 1883–1884 | Taught at Hutchinson Charity School in Paisley. |
| 1884 | October 23, married Margaret Cameron MacArthur of Perth, daughter of John MacArthur, owner of a bobbin factory, one-time mayor of Perth. |
| 1884–1885 | Clerk in a Glasgow thread company. |
| 1885 | Published his first novel, *The North Wall* (Glasgow), and his verse drama, *Diabolus Amans* (Glasgow). |
| 1885–1888 | Taught at Morrison's Academy at Crieff. |
| 1887 | Son Alexander born (d. 1940). |
| 1888–1889 | Taught in a private school in Greenock. |
| 1889 | Son Menzies born (d. about 1960). |
| 1890 | Gave up teaching; moved with his family to London to take up full-time literary career. Became reviewer, critic, and hack writer. |
| 1891 | Subeditor of a short-lived periodical, *Weekly Review*. |
| 1891 ff. | Friendship or acquaintance with most of the London literary and publishing world—W. B. Yeats, Grant Allen, Edmund Gosse, Arthur Symons, James Barrie, W. E. Henley. |
| c. 1891–1894 | Member in good standing of the Rhymers' Club. |
| 1893 | April, *Fleet Street Eclogues* published; Davidson's first success, went to a second edition in three months. |
| 1893–1899 | Association with the publishing firm of Elkin Matthews and John Lane, the Bodley Head. |

| | |
|---|---|
| 1894 | Contributed to *Yellow Book*; published *Ballads and Songs*, his best and most famous work. |
| 1896 | February 27 to May 30, Davidson's adaptation of François Coppée's *Pour la Couronne* staged with some success. |
| 1896– 1897 and 1897– 1898 | Spent winters alone at Shoreham, Sussex, in order to have time to read and write. Probably first real acacquaintance with the writings of Nietzsche. |
| 1900 | William Symington McCormick and Edmund Gosse tried without success to get Davidson a pension. |
| 1901 | With publication of *Self's the Man*, began the association with the publisher Grant Richards which continued until Davidson's death. Publications of the first of Davidson's five Testaments, *The Testament of a Vivisector*, marked the beginning of the explicitly materialistic writings. |
| c. 1901 | G. B. Shaw commissioned Davidson to write a play for which Davidson received £250. The resulting play, which Shaw described as "not popular enough for a popular theatre; and . . . not advanced enough for a coterie theatre," was never produced; has been lost. |
| 1905 | Publication of the play, *The Theatrocrat*, brought Davidson a storm of adverse criticism, which in turn brought the critics a storm of abuse in the form of letters to the editor from Davidson. |
| 1906 | Davidson got £100 annual Civil List Pension. |
| 1907 | On April 11, his fiftieth birthday, published a play, *The Triumph of Mammon*, the first volume of a projected trilogy to be entitled "God and Mammon." Left London with his family in June for Penzance on the coast of Cornwall. |
| 1908 | February, wrote to Richards: "I should like to leave my affairs in some shape behind me: I have had very distinct notice that I have barely a year or two to live in now." September 1, Grant Richards agreed to pay Davidson about £100 a year for being his "literary adviser" and a reader of manuscripts. Publication of *The* |

*Testament of John Davidson,* the last book published while he was alive.

1909    March 23, 6:30 P.M., Davidson left his home at 6 Coulson's Terrace, Penzance, never to return. Footprints were found leading from a path to the edge of a cliff at the seashore. Saturday, September 18, two Mousehole fishermen found a body which Menzies Davidson identified as his father's. Tuesday, September 21, Davidson's body was buried at sea. *Fleet Street and other Poems* published with Davidson's suicide note as the preface: "The time has come to make an end. . . ."

# CHAPTER 1

# *"Find My Development in My Books"*

> "He had got rid of his Scotch accent, but he couldn't get rid of his Scotch nature."
> —John Davidson, *Laura Ruthven's Widowhood*

AFTER John Davidson disappeared on March 23, 1909, his family found in his will the charge that "no one is to write my life now or at any time; but let all men study and discuss in private and in public my poems and my plays, especially my Testaments and Tragedies."[1] For a long time the first part of his injunction was honored; Davidson's life was not written until 1961, except for brief biographical notices such as that in the *Dictionary of National Biography*. But we cannot by any stretch of the imagination say that the rest of Davidson's wish was honored. Instead of all men's reading his "Testaments and Tragedies," few have bothered to read Davidson at all; or, if they did, they read the lyrics and ballads of the 1890's, not the apocalyptic writings of the final years.

## I  *Religion, Rebellion, and Science*

Since this is not another life of Davidson, I have put what I consider important factual data into the chronology. There are, nevertheless, two important points about Davidson's early life which should be stressed. The first is of special significance in understanding the growth of Davidson's mind: his Scotch Protestant Evangelicalism. Growing up with strict Evangelical parents leaves its indelible mark on any boy, and the effect is greater when the boy has a Scotch Evangelical minister for a father, as did John. Evangelical as he was, Davidson would have grown up with a need for a belief. For the Evangelical, belief, not morality or ethics, is of first importance, though the pietism that accompanies Evangelicalism often makes great pretenses of concern with morality. Once he assents to his beliefs, the Evangelical finds great security in them because, for all practical purposes, every important question is answered with utter finality either by dogma or by literal interpretation of the Bible—the "paper pope," Karl Barth calls it. Thus the Evangelical depends very heavily upon his beliefs for mental stability; and, though he may in later life rebel against the narrowness of the Evangelical creeds and dogmas and may reject all those comfortable answers to the problems of existence, he still has the nagging, even peremptory, yearning for a creed to hold to. As R. M. Wenley, philosopher and fellow Scot, says of Davidson, "He never permits himself to forget that dogma gone or going must be replaced by dogma come or coming." [2]

And, if the Evangelical needs a dogma, he needs almost as much to be dogmatic, to be a missionary. "Go ye into all the world and preach the gospel" is an exhortation taken literally by a good Evangelical, one which Davidson's minister father obviously took to heart, and which, we suspect from Davidson's dedication to art for teaching's sake, the son also adopted. Though he chose to preach a secular gospel, the moral earnestness and missionary-mindedness of the Evangelical were unmistakably part of Davidson's nature. Even as an unregenerate, Davidson was almost fated to teach, to preach, even to prophesy—as were Thomas Carlyle and George Eliot, both ex-Evangelicals and both earnest moralists.

The Evangelical's tendencies toward dogma and dogmatizing are only one side of the picture, however. On the other side is the passionate Evangelical nonconformist, the questioner. Dogmatic, yes, but at the same time the Evangelical wholeheartedly embraces Paul's injunction to be not conformed to this world, not even to be conformed to dogma if it comes to that; and the twelve or fifteen secessions that occurred in the Scottish Protestant church between 1690 and 1900 testify to the power of this concept.[3] The conscience is the final arbiter in matters of belief, a higher authority than dogma or the church. Davidson inherited an overflowing measure of the temper of Scotch Protestantism.

Thus it is with Davidson as it is with his fictional character Scotchman Leonard Brandon in the novel *Laura Ruthven's Widowhood*: "He had got rid of his Scotch accent, but he couldn't get rid of his Scotch nature." [4] Of course, we are on shaky ground when we generalize about national characteristics, but we are not saying that Davidson has Scottish *racial* characteristics but that

Davidson, growing up in the home of a Scottish Protestant Evangelical preacher, rightfully came by certain distinctive cultural characteristics, which are traceable to Evangelicalism in general and to Scottish Evangelicalism in particular.

As we have noted, Davidson was always an Evangelical who needed a belief for peace of mind. Harold Williams says of him, "Like Carlyle he was a protagonist of the actual, for in boyhood he had been trained in the strictest sect of the Calvinists, and like Carlyle he spent half his life buffeting the universe as a Calvinist without dogma." [5] In spite of Davidson's attempt during the 1890's to maintain philosophic detachment toward all dogma, he had to utter his everlasting yea to something; as it turned out, it was his own special brand of materialism mixed with heroic vitalism. Taking his Evangelical upbringing into account, Davidson's earnest, almost pious, dedication to art with a message is no surprise. Particularly in the final years (1901–9) in the Testaments and Mammon plays, Davidson preaches, and sometimes passionately prophesies, with the conviction of an evangelist or a revivalist. In the iconoclasm of the earliest works there is evidence of the moralist's vehemence, and even in the relatively restrained writings of the 1890's one occasionally hears the voice of one crying in the wilderness.

Davidson's perfervid nonconformity and resultant self-dependence are also part of his Scottish religious and cultural heritage. It is no accident that Bruce and Wallace figure in his early heroic drama, *Bruce* (1886); for Davidson grew up in the environment where, as J. Benjamin Townsend says, "Wallace first defied the English . . . Bruce set out for Bannockburn, and on its wild moorlands gathered the Convenanters who in the seventeenth century renounced allegiance to the Stuarts." [6] Rebellion and independence were as much a part of Davidson's religio-cultural heritage as were dogma and dogmatism, and his unceasing questioning of received values is as much a part of him as his need for the security of a creed. Like the heroic-materialistic philosophy which he advocates in the final works, Davidson's Scottish Protestant Evangelicalism is paradoxical in nature.

If the first pertinent point about Davidson's biography, then, is the large degree of Scottish Evangelicalism which he assimilated from the environment of his formative years, the second pertinent point is more difficult to substantiate, since there is little biographical information and Davidson is silent on the subject. During his adolescence, Davidson was strongly influenced by the scientific and materialistic thought of the later nineteenth century.

Sometime in 1870, Davidson, who was then thirteen, left school to work in the chemical laboratory of Walker's, one of Greenock's great sugarhouses. A year later he put his experience to good account by becoming assistant to the public analyst in Greenock, a responsible job for a fourteen-year-old boy. He stayed at this second job for about a year, so that altogether he had two years' experience as a practical, working scientist. Of course, we cannot say for certain what effects this experience had on the boy, but it is quite possible that he would have found the atmosphere in the laboratory quite intellectually stimulating compared to the confines of his Evangelical home. We may safely assume that he had as co-workers and supervisors men who were enthusiastically interested in the things that were then taking place in science. This period was, after all, only eleven years after Charles Darwin's *Origin of Species* and only two years after Thomas Henry Huxley's essay "On the Physical Basis of Life" had appeared in the *Fortnightly Review*.

In short, the great conflict between science and religion (which is still by no means dead) was raging nearly at its height; and in the laboratory Davidson may well have heard a good deal of argument on the side of science. In any case, his later writings show that he had carefully read Darwin, Huxley, and Herbert Spencer (which he could have done without the laboratory experience); and he may well have found a good deal to admire in the scientific method, if nothing else. He found much in Darwinism to satirize (see the discussion of *Earl Lavender* in Chapter 3), but Davidson's measure of the nature of God and the universe is based on a sort of empiricism: only so much of God as he can personally perceive will he believe in, he says in his early confessional poem, *Diabolus Amans* (see Chapter 2).

Furthermore, Davidson's materialism in the later works shows a distinctly scientific bias; but he arrives at his hypotheses intuitively rather than empirically. Nonetheless, Davidson's last works are full of scientific jargon; as Douglas Bush says of the *Testament of John Davidson* (1908), "A reader may lose his way amid whirling words and electrons." [7] Much scientific (or pseudoscientific) material is included in Davidson's materialistic cosmography.

Whether the scientific, empirical, and factual elements in David-son's thought can be traced to his two years in the chemical lab-oratory is, in the absence of biographical or textual data, highly conjectural; but the technological experience is worth noting and considering in his final affirmation of materialism. Two years of experience as a practicing scientist must have been crucial in form-ing his attitudes toward science and religion.

Despite the fact that data do not do much to explain Davidson, they do suggest some reasons why he was such an ardent disbe-liever and why he eventually finally believed in something. And they do account to some extent for his interest in science. But the process by which he arrived at his strange philosophy is not thereby set forth or interpreted satisfactorily.

## II  *Central Themes*

How can Davidson's odyssey from Evangelicalism to material-ism and finally suicide be explained? Davidson himself has furnished what I believe is the best clue to the means of under-standing his growth as a poet and thinker. In answer to Cornelius Weygandt, who had written him in 1897 asking him for informa-tion regarding his educational influences and his development, Davidson wrote: "As for development, is it not the open secret of every poet's writing, ready, indeed eager, to yield itself to the attentive student? *My readers must find my development in my books.*" [8] That is the purpose of this study: to follow Davidson's advice to find his development by making a careful survey of his books, as well as his other writings, published and unpublished.

There are two central themes which run through all Davidson's writings and around which his ideas cluster: the first of these cen-tral themes is Davidson's concern for problems of belief. As he tries to solve these problems, he goes from rejection of Christianity to philosophic detachment to a firm assent to materialism. The second of these central themes arises from his interest in hero worship and heroic vitalism, for he moves from youthful rebel-liousness to hero worship to celebration of an English "superman." And, in the final Testaments and Mammon plays, he tries to syn-thesize these two seemingly antithetical themes into a kind of poetic-heroic-materialistic view of the universe. Thus, by examin-ing Davidson's treatment of these two central ideas, we may trace the development of his ideas as well as the utilization of various literary forms to convey his ideas.

Davidson's development falls into three periods, which seemingly have their parallel in the spiritual biographies of many nineteenth-century writers: (1) the years to 1890, during which he shouted his everlasting no at religion and conventionality; (2) the decade from 1890 to 1900, when he tried, as much as lay in him, to exist in a center of indifference, or irony, as he called it; and (3) the final years 1901–1909, which began suddenly, though not too surprisingly, with a resounding everlasting yea to hero worship and to materialistic philosophy and which ended in suicide.

In Davidson's development one finds a veritable compendium of the crosscurrents of late nineteenth-century thought—almost, as he puts it himself, "a mouthpiece for the creeds of all the world." Thus, we study in Davidson not only his development but that of a singularly contradictory and enigmatic period of literary and intellectual history. From Davidson we can learn about the questions raised during those years—they are the ones we ask—as well as about the answers proposed; for Davidson was first and foremost a humanist and his concerns are humane. From him, we may learn about ourselves.

# CHAPTER 2

# The Early Period: 1877-1889

> His guiding star
> Is that same beacon of rebellious light
> Built up by every burning Scottish heart.
> —John Davidson, *Bruce*, 1884

BEFORE John Davidson came to London in 1890 to begin a full-time literary career, he had already published five plays, a long dramatic poem, and a novel.[1] A volume of poems, *In a Music-Hall and other Poems*, though not published until 1891, was ready for publication as early as 1884.[2] In these early writings are to be found many of the themes which Davidson developed in his mature writings.

## I. *Early Iconoclasm*: An Unhistorical Pastoral *and* A Romantic Farce

According to Davidson's dating, the earliest of his works is a play, *An Unhistorical Pastoral*, written in 1877.[3] Highly derivative, it is a drama of romantic love treated with Elizabethan exuberance, with plot situations and diction culled from Shakespeare and other Elizabethan poets. However, *A Romantic Farce*, written in 1878, though not published until 1889,[4] is less derivative and is more typical of Davidson. The action of the play begins at a masked ball, where one of the maskers, known only as the Courtier (he is a writer, we learn), proposes to the other maskers that they wear their disguises the next day to see what might happen. In this courtier, we meet the first of many heroes who seem to be dramatic projections of the author and mouthpieces for his ideas. The writer-courtier reinforces his proposal with a very typical Davidsonian outburst:

> Fashion, propriety, convention?—Tush!
> Let us like noble heretics protest

Against all dogmas false and fashionable,
...........  ..............................................................

Then, gentle friends, since such is our resolve,
We can do nothing nobler than attack
Fashion's mainstay, the discipline of dress.

Unfortunately, what could be a very intriguing plot situation for a "romantic farce" is all but forgotten. The characters pass the remainder of their time in the forest, and the upshot of it is that various long-lost lovers, mothers, fathers, and wives are discovered, and everyone who is not already married gets married. What begins as a "Romantic" drama of protest turns, therefore, into mere romancing. Nevertheless, the courtier who objectifies Davidson's early rejection of determinism and his belief in the freedom of the will and the possibility of full self-development is an important foreshadowing of the hero as dramatized in his works of the 1890's as well as the superman heroes of the plays of the later period. The admiration of strength in the face of hostile fate inevitably calls to mind Thomas Carlyle and Robert Browning, as well as Alfred Lord Tennyson, especially as he was, for example, the poet of manliness in such a poem as "Ulysses." The courtier's ideas are surely an anticipation of W. E. Henley's vitalism in "Invictus," though I do not mean to suggest that A Romantic Farce influenced Henley.

Davidson's admiration for his contemporaries that we have just mentioned can be easily illustrated from a letter written to Algernon Swinburne in 1879, asking for encouragement and assistance: "Were I a member of Parliament I would bring in a bill to establish a new order of merit, to consist of four members only and always: the title would be the absence of all title, and the first four members Swinburne, Tennyson, Browning (Pervervidum Scotorum), Carlyle." [5] Even if we discount the youthful extravagance of the letter, it helps to establish Davidson's debts to Carlyle, Browning, and Tennyson, the admirers of strength and manliness, as well as to Swinburne, the iconoclast.

## II  *Heroism:* Bruce

Six years passed before the writing of *Bruce: a Chronicle Play,* 1884.[6] In it Davidson glorifies Robert Bruce, Scotland's greatest hero and the epitome of Scotch rebelliousness. The Battle of Bannockburn, after which the English never again conquered Scotland, is the subject of the last act of the play. Using the technique of his master Shakespeare, Davidson follows the general outlines of the career of Bruce; but he also feels free to rearrange history to serve the purposes of the drama.

Davidson's Bruce has a large sense of workaday practicality, which, coupled with the restiveness of his spirit, makes him a successful rebel-hero. Edward I says of Bruce in the opening speech of the play, "He goes to Scotland, and his guiding star/Is that same beacon of rebellious light/Built up by every burning Scottish heart." After Bruce's "guiding star" has led him to murder his rival Comyn, Bruce justifies his deed as not premeditated; it was instinctive self-assertiveness. Bruce the hero trusts intuition; for example, he answers his own conscience, the voice of maturity, in this way:

> Now,
> Right in thy teeth, or in thy toothless chaps,
> I swear, antiquity, first thoughts are best:
> Their treble notes I still shall hearken to,
> And let no second, murmuring soft, seduce
> Their clear and forthright meaning.

(147)

This sort of dependence upon emotion and intuition is one of the characteristics of a typical Davidson hero; and in a long succession of such heroic characters we find eventually Davidson himself in the hero's role in *The Testament of John Davidson* in 1908. These heroes are proud and independent; they revere emotion and feeling more than intellect and rational thought. Often they openly reject determinism and Victorian ennui in their attempts to assert their personalities upon their environments. For example, the whole play *Bruce* testifies to its hero's practical genius in changing circumstances so as to bring about the defeat of the English. And it testifies also to Bruce's colossal egoism and faith in his own abilities.

Undoubtedly there is a Carlylean influence on Davidson's concept of the heroic character. Bruce is a very good example of the Carlylean hero, except that perhaps he is not quite "universal" enough to take his place alongside Carlyle's heroes—Luther or Knox, for example. Nevertheless, Bruce is a doer, an activist, a practical man. In trusting himself, he carries out the duty which is imposed upon him by the Scottish people. Like a true Carlylean hero, Bruce is a product of his time, but he also transcends the spirit of his time and brings about great and momentous change. Thus, while Davidson's thoughts about the hero and heroic behavior undergo many changes, and he even at times satirizes the hero, Bruce remains an outstanding example of the sort of Davidson hero that ultimately is transfigured into a superman in the later works.

## IV  *Rejection of Christianity:* Diabolus Amans

In 1885, Davidson's *Diabolus Amans: A Dramatic Poem* appeared anonymously in Glasgow.[7] Not quite a drama, it is a series of nine scenes, more or less dramatic, but unified by ideas, not by a single action. In any case, *Diabolus Amans* is the central document of the early period, for it is a statement of Davidson's faith, a sort of personal testimony, to use the language of the Evangelical church from which he broke away. Furthermore, it reflects fully his spiritual struggles, his wavering between belief and unbelief, idealism and materialism.

The problem which the poet ostensibly sets out to solve in *Diabolus Amans* is suggested in the title, and this was printed as a motto opposite the title page: "What if the Devil were a man in love,/ And loved a woman good as women be/ Who are not wicked;—what's the sequel, say?" (2). In the poem itself, this question is first posed by the hero, a poet named Angelus, at a "wine party" in his rooms. After the others leave the party, Angelus, responding to his own question, begins to make it clear that he is the devil in love. He has a sinful past which haunts him over and over again (Diabolus), and we learn in Scene 2 that he is in love (amans) with a girl named Donna. During their second encounter in the poem, the thesis question is answered when Donna asks, "Could any be Diabolus and love,/ Or loving could he be Diabolus?," Angelus replies: "He could not love and be Diabolus;/ The more a being loves the less he sins;/ And perfect love were perfect purity" (57).

The poet takes human love to be evidence of the spiritual in man and therefore of God in the universe, a sort of "I love, therefore I believe" formula. It seems that Davidson is trying to tell us that literally "God *is* love" and that also "Love *is* God." This method of perceiving God is based not on theological reasoning, not on faith or creeds or divine revelation, but on the emotions of love: " 'Tis the heart that apprehends/ Immortal verities and not the brain" (63). It is a Romantic and existential view of God, as we would say,[8] or, to put it another way, it is a sort of empiricism: because I experience love, I can accept a God who is love.

Although these quotations seem to indicate that human love is a sufficient basis for belief in God, Angelus has by no means said all that he has to say on the subject of belief. Along with his sinful past, he still must exorcise the demons of creedal Christianity which haunt him, especially those of Protestant Evangelicalism; and he must restate the creeds of his personal faith. Furthermore, though he professes over and over his denial of dogma, he is intensely concerned with spiritual regeneration, the problem of atoning for his sins. The remainder of the poem (more than half of it) is related not to the immediate question of what the Devil would do if he were in love, but to what that Devil will do now that he has in effect been "converted."

It soon becomes clear that the first thing the Devil will do is inform us in no uncertain terms that he cannot be bound by religious creeds. For example, in Scene 4, which is set in an Evangelical church in France (why France I do not know), Angelus specifically rejects Protestant Evangelicalism and, in fact, much of orthodox Christian theology. Nevertheless, Angelus admits his sinfulness: "Ay, once I sinned a sin that was a sin. . . . I knew in other phrase, that sin *is* sin,/ And he who sinneth hath begun to die" (74–75). Although Angelus is an orthodox sinner, he cannot accept the orthodox means of redemption. He scornfully refers to the crucifixion as a sign of God's injustice, "a murder foul,/ The death of innocence for guilt" (76). But, if Davidson can be the Devil's advocate, he can do as well or better as the advocate of traditional Christianity. As though hearing Angelus' criticism, the Pastor counters with the ancient question: "Man, who art thou that thou shouldst answer God?" Angelus cannot answer God; instead, he resorts to a denunciation of orthodoxy. The passage which follows is, until 1885, Davidson's most thorough everlasting no to creedal belief:

> Once for all,
> In rite or dogma flourished as divine,
> Whate'er offends the taste and shocks the sense,

And quarrels with the tints of Earth and Sky,—
Whate'er is prose, and is not poetry,
Father of Lies, I relegate to thee,
And I will none of it: that rag and paste,
That papery sentiment, those stuccoed saints,
Those "stations" coloured ill and ill-bestowed,
That gilt o'erlaid with dirt most catholic,
That manufactured wafer,—not for me!
—I am a poet! and the soul of all
Hath sacraments more fitting; Sea and Sky,
These are the symbols of the Infinite,
These are the letters of the Everlasting.
                                                    (79–80) 9

In the first ten lines of the quotation Davidson puts his finger very precisely on one mistake which institutional religion often makes; it confuses the symbol and the thing symbolized. The last four lines of the quotation summarize Davidson's new set of symbols of faith: what we might call poetic experience is at the heart of his belief. Like Carlyle or the early Wordsworth, he looks upon nature as the garment of God; sea and sky are more fitting embodiments of God, or sacraments, as he calls them, than are the conventional sacraments of Christianity. In another passage, he sets forth his "supernatural naturalism" (Angelus is speaking to Donna); and Davidson seems to have him say that Being is the ground for belief.

Yes, I believe He is because I am,
That as my body and mine outward life
Are sacramental solely of a self
Invisible and real, so this, the world
I gaze on, this material universe,
Is but the sacrament of soul, and else
Nothing, unmeaning and irrelevant.
                                                    (59–60)

Davidson does not deny the reality of the universe, or of his body and his outward self; but, as a poet, he is aware that they are symbols of some deeper spiritual reality, something he vaguely calls "soul." Whatever it is, this "soul" gives meaning and relevance to a universe that would otherwise be "nothing," but he does not go so far as to say that it would not exist: it would be nothing in the sense of having no value, no meaning, no relationship to some higher unknown. In any case, Davidson is assuredly not at this point a materialist; he is (if I must label him) a sort of neo-Platonist or perhaps a Wordsworthian.

Other poetic experiences, or psychic phenomena, one might say, are basic to Davidson's belief in God. Poetic inspiration, a kind of divine afflatus, is evidence of God. Furthermore, because he is a poet, Angelus has no difficulty in believing in the resurrection, or the idea of immortality which hinges on resurrection. He has mystical experiences,[10] he tells Donna; and in these he transcends all the limits of time, space, and his human nature: "I was God, I was Eternity" (64), he says of one such experience.

Just what the nature of God is that Angelus identifies himself with is very difficult to say. In any case, Davidson's belief is established on the grounds of a purely personal perception of God, not on the grounds of revealed scriptures, faith, or theological systems. In some respects, his belief is close to the intuitionism of the Deists. His outlook is empiricist, for his knowledge of God extends only as far as his own experience of God leads him. He does not take God on faith but on the facts of poetic experience.

Angelus, having settled for himself and Donna the question of the basis for his belief in God, seriously sets about to find the means of atoning for his sins. He has already rejected the orthodox atonement through the blood of Christ, but he cannot reject the need for expiation. He seems constrained somehow to work out his salvation with fear and trembling. For a time, Angelus toys with the idea that salvation comes through the purgations of pain and suffering in this life. He concludes, however, that sins cannot be expiated simply by fighting the good fight against fate. In the end, Angelus turns to good works:

> To dream of happiness was too absurd,
> To help a little in the happiness
> Of others,—that, no more, was left to me
> And that I found at first a sedative,
> And then a tonic.
>
> (107–8)

Thus, Davidson has discovered a basis of atonement which he later describes as "the heresy of 'works'" (137). In this change of emphasis from theology to ethics, Davidson was doing what other Protestant modernists did during the last decades of the nineteenth century. In accepting Darwinism and in discarding historic Christian dogma, the modernists shifted their attention from faith to good works.[11] Angelus explains to Donna the "heresy" of works rather than faith:

> Sound the philosophy—*believe and live;*
> *Live and believe* were just as sound, I wis;
> If faith precede or works, or if the twain
> Shall run abreast, ay, be discovered one,
> I know not, care not, this, at least, I know:—
> Wouldst thou believe in God, thou must be good.[12]
>
> (109)

*Diabolus Amans* is the Testament of John Davidson, 1885 version. As we have seen, it is his statement of belief and unbelief. Davidson says that the devil could not be a man in love; for "he may not love and be Diabolus." Love then is one basis for belief, or at least for joining the side of the angels. Anxious as Davidson is to establish his unconventionality, he sweeps aside all creedal and dogmatic systems. In the final pages of the poem, Angelus reiterates his contempt for creeds and his dislike of theological niceties. Of theology, he says,

> I rather listen to the scientist
> —Inspired interpreter of holy writ,
> Why then the mountain burns with fire and smoke,
> Till all I see and all I touch is God,
> And science seems the true theology.
>
> (137–38)

As a way of explaining the material universe, science is more efficient than theology, just as personal experience is a better basis for belief than faith. Theology, as the study of divine things or of religious truth, ought to be based on observation of nature rather than on a supposedly revealed scripture, the authenticity of which Davidson questions repeatedly. The empirical tendencies of this argument parallel the empiricism of Davidson's belief in God—a God apprehended through various personal experiences such as love, poetic inspiration, or mystical states. In its skepticism and

[ 26 ]

empiricism, Davidson's state of mind in 1885 surely points forward to the fully materialistic synthesis of the last years of his life. His apparent partiality to science, which in 1885 would imply Darwinism in some one of its forms, confirms the possibility of an ultimate materialism.

Nevertheless, we must conclude from the evidence of the poem that Davidson is not yet committed to materialism—at least, not consciously. A combination of religious skepticism, empiricism, and belief in science may be leading the way; but Davidson clearly still clings to spiritual realities that cannot be explained physically —love, immortality, and poetic ecstasy. Nature is still supernatural. It still embodies the spiritual reality beneath.

### IV   *Problems of the Artist:* The North Wall

Near the end of *Diabolus Amans,* Angelus is explaining to Donna something about the sinfulness of his early life before love had transformed him. He was a writer, unable to accept Christianity, who made art a religion:

> So left, without the consecrating sense
> Of sympathy sublime, I, in my search
> Of matter for the novel or the play,
> I lived the thing I wrote;—even the crimes:
> Behold me then committed to a course,
> The future all foreclosed, or ere I saw
> The folly of it.
>
> (136)

Thus, it seems that Angelus' sin was part of the *mal de siècle*: "art for art's sake" carried to the extreme of confusing art with life, or what we may call "life for art's sake."

This sort of aesthetic sin is the subject of Davidson's first novel, *The North Wall,* 1885.[13] "The novel is all played out," says Maxwell Lee, the hero. "I am going to create a novel. Practical joking is the new novel in its infancy. The end of every thought is an action; and the centuries of written fiction must culminate in an age of acted fiction." Lee then explains his method: "Novel-writing is effete; novel-creation is about to begin. We shall cause a novel to take place in the world. We shall construct a plot; we shall select a hero; we shall enter into his life, and produce the series of events before determined on" (9–10).

Lee is able to try out his new method when a well-to-do business man, Henry Chartres, is injured and knocked unconscious in a carriage accident and is brought to Lee's house by Briscoe. Briscoe, Lee's brother-in-law, intends to get Chartres' money; but Lee has other plans. Fortunately for his plot, Chartres looks a good deal like Lee; furthermore, Lee discovers by reading letters in Chartres' possession that Chartres is just arriving home after a ten-year absence. Thus Lee is able to assume the person of Chartres and to practice his manipulation of life on the members of the Chartres household at Snell House, or he does so at least until Chartres regains consciousness and freedom.

It soon becomes clear to the reader that Davidson is satirizing the Romantic esthete for whom art exists *in vacuo*, for whom art is totally separated from the bounds of common sense, morality, or conventionality. Lee answers his wife's moral objection to imprisoning Chartres:

At the start of this new departure in the art of fiction we will be much hampered in its exercise by scruples and fears of this kind. Some of us may even require to be martyrs. . . . Once the veracity and nobility, the magnanimity and self-sacrifice which shall characterize this art and the professors of it, have raised the tone of the world, we shall be granted, I doubt not, the most cordial permission to execute atrocities which, committed selfishly, would brand the criminal as an unnatural monster, but which performed for art's sake, will redound everlastingly to the credit of the artist.

(17–18)

This statement illustrates what we might call the principle of "crime for art's sake"; without doubt, it is a satiric portrayal of the artistic position which Angelus, in *Diabolus Amans,* confesses as having been his sin. Like the hero of Oscar Wilde's *Dorian Gray,* the hero of *The North Wall* represents the amoral artist; he is concerned purely with artistic effect and feels no compunction about injuries, physical or psychological, which he may cause. On the other hand, Lee is anxious to "raise the tone" at Snell House, to intensify emotions, and to vivify experience. As things turn out, however, Lee causes very little damage to anyone's person or psyche; moreover, events develop in their own way, in spite of his attempts at being the *deus ex machina.*

[ 28 ]

Davidson's other important object of satire in *The North Wall* is himself as artist. The hero, Maxwell Lee, is in many ways similar to Davidson. Lee, like Davidson, is an unsuccessful literary man (9); he has written "dramas and philosophical romances [*Diabolus Amans*?]" (10). Like Davidson, Lee is a Scot, and the setting is Greenock where Davidson lived and worked from 1870 to 1877. Even more convincing are the parallels in thinking: Lee regards love as sacredly as Davidson, in spite of his professed amorality (38, 55). Lee says that his presence in the Chartres household is providing "the dash of bitter that strengthens the sweet; the need for rebellion that wakens the soul; the spur that drives nature rough-shod over conventions" (98). That assertion expresses Davidsonian rebelliousness, yet Lee and his activities and ideas are obviously the object of satire. How may this self-parody be explained?

As I have shown, Davidson has given a firm denial to religious creeds of all kinds, and in *A Romantic Farce* to conventions in general. Although we have seen that Davidson still holds to some canons of morality, he has been moving away from any well-defined norm of regular behavior, or from what we call "conventions." Completely skeptical about established modes of belief, the things he does accept are based on the authority of his own perceptions. Thus Davidson's attitude toward received beliefs and values is that of ironic detachment. The same detachment, carried one step further, can bring detached scrutiny to bear upon his own beliefs. After all, since he has no basis for his own beliefs except his personal experience, he can question the authority of his own mind just as he questions any imposed authority. The ironist mocks, therefore, at the convictions of the believer, even when the believer is himself. In a world of shifting values, he cannot even believe in his own standards of values.[14] There is, of course, a paradox involved in my explanation: belief and disbelief can exist in the same person concerning the same subject. But the reader cannot deny that the portrait of the artist in *The North Wall* is paradoxical. Perhaps we must explain a paradox with a paradox.[15]

We may conclude that, by the time he wrote *The North Wall*, around 1885, Davidson had rejected "art for art's sake"; but, because of his irony, his attitude is surely ambiguous. Nevertheless, by showing that events at Snell House work out just as they no doubt would have if Lee had not interfered, Davidson is implying that he questions not only the ability of the Esthete to make life follow art but also the worth of "art for art's sake." We can indeed go further and say that Davidson questions the effectiveness of art of any kind. Lee believes that he has "raised the tone" at Snell House, but there is no evidence that he has done anything more than interfere, for he has most assuredly not changed anyone's mind on any subject whatever. Thus, Davidson's attitude toward art is as ironical as his attitude toward himself. He takes it seriously and laughs at it at the same time. He practices it but does not believe in its power to produce effects, either as "art for art's sake" or as art for morality or for instruction.

In the ballad, "The Gleeman," from *In A Music-Hall*, Davidson expresses the same doubts by depicting a minstrel singing in the marketplace; the old women notice his clothes, the young women his curls, the old men his youth, but no one listens to his song. Yet, when he leaves, the juggler, the mountebank, and the pardoner, all quacks, find a ready reception.[16] In another ballad from the same volume, "Thomas the Rhymer," Davidson tells of Thomas, a poet-seer, whose prophecy goes unheeded.[17] Thus, there is a good deal of evidence that in these crucial years in Davidson's career— a few years before he gave up teaching to devote himself to writing full time—he was deeply concerned with the role of the artist and with the problem of gaining an audience, an audience which every sort of quack can command but one which ignores the poet and his Cassandra-like message. Because Davidson obviously has misgivings about the value of art, it is difficult to account for his great devotion to it. Nevertheless, in spite of his own ironic self-awareness, he seems to favor the idea that art should exist for the sake of ideas; for "art for art's sake" is a formula which he has outgrown. Again, Davidson apparently takes refuge in a paradox: though he remains uncertain about the value of art, he is a dedicated practitioner.

### V  Heroism, Iconoclasm, and the Problems of the Artist: Smith *and* Scaramouch

The character of the poet and his search for an audience are central themes in Davidson's next work, the play, *Smith: a Tragic Farce*, written in 1886.[18] The subtitle indicates Davidson's ironic detachment toward the artist and his problems. He is, on the one hand, tragically involved in the suicide deaths of the two heroes;

on the other hand, he is aware of the farcical elements in their melodramatic posturings. The play is also a fearful portent of Davidson's literary career: a provincial comes to London, fails as a writer, and commits suicide rather than resign to fate.

The two heroes of *Smith* are projections of Davidson. It is not clear what Smith's profession is, except that he is a "thinker," but Hallowes is an "out-at-elbows" poet, a former schoolteacher who found teaching "shameful pedagogy" and "mental bootblacking" and who is no happier in business—"the sale of lies"—than in teaching.[19] Smith, like Davidson, is a provincial, "uncultured, too; he lacks the college stamp." He shares Davidson's habit of denouncing conventionality:

> I would rather be
> A shred of glass that sparkles in the sun,
> And keeps a lowly rainbow of its own,
> Than one of those so trim and patent pearls
> With hearts of sand veneered, sewed up and down
> The stiff brocade society affects.
>
> (224–25)

Thus Hallowes and Smith represent, respectively, Davidson the poet and Davidson the thinker. From their subsequent brief careers, we can learn something of Davidson's thoughts about these two facets of his character.

Smith and Hallowes decide to spend a holiday at Garth in the north of England, seeking solace in an escape from the city to Nature. There, Hallowes says, he will write poetry, "a line a day,/ If nothing more" (228); and he hopes that his poetry will bring him fame and renown. When Smith warns him of the dangers involved in the search for fame, Hallowes argues that nothing— whether it be war, politics, or art—is practiced for itself but for fame and power; and "fame is worth its cost," he says (228). Smith's statement of his argument is a classic example of the language of heroic vitalism: "But you are right; one must become/ Fanatic—be a wedge—a thunderbolt,/ To smite a passage through the close-grained world" (230).

Hallowes' literary pilgrimage to Garth ends in failure. The pastoral beauty fails to arouse his creative energy, and his productions are "returned with thanks" from London (233). Rather than continue fighting for recognition, he climbs to the top of Mount Merlin at Garth, opens a vein, and dies slowly while uttering a long soliloquy about the loss of creative power and about death in a fashion which calls to mind Matthew Arnold's dramatic poem *Empedocles on Etna* (1852). Thus the poet in Davidson (Hallowes) escapes in suicide his own failures and his unappreciative audiences. As I will note later, to Davidson suicide is not merely an escape but also a kind of perverse victory.

Smith, who in this play represents Davidson the thinker (perhaps synonymous with Davidson the Protestant), is meanwhile in love with Magdalen, who is to be married against her will to Brown, a London acquaintance of Smith. Smith, practicing what he preaches about being a fanatic, a wedge, a thunderbolt, urges her to be as unconventional as he is. She is; and, accepting Smith as "the strong deliverer/ To pluck her from the dragon's jaws unharmed" (236), she consents to elope with her deliverer to London. Smith is forceful, as we have seen: he is, according to Brown who arrives on the scene, "the kind of man that healthy girls/ Yield to at once" (244). And yield she does; at least she yields to his desire to elope with her against the wishes of her father and her fiancé.

When authority in the person of Magdalen's father Graham interposes, Smith argues that their love has made Magdalen a queen. But her father has planned a good marriage for his daughter for years, and Smith is in his eyes no good. Thwarted, the lovers attempt to seal for eternity this moment of great love which the philistine (and, one is tempted to add, sensible) world would spoil. Smith explains his actions:

> Yes, we can go where none will follow us,
> We two could never love each other more
> Than now we do. . . .
> I have a million things to tell my love,
> But I will keep them for eternity.
> Good earth, good mother earth, my mate and me—
> Take us.
>
> (248)

And he leaps with Magdalen over a precipice. Twenty-three years later, Davidson ended his life by jumping into the sea at Penzance.

Although this reference is the first of many in Davidson's works to suicide as an escape from a hostile world and at the same time a heroic triumph over it, there are earlier references to death (not necessarily by suicide) as a final act of heroism or escape. In *The North Wall*, Lee, the hero, tells his accomplice Briscoe that death for him would be both a release and a triumph.[20] And in *Diabolus Amans*, Donna, in the ecstasy of her new-found love for Angelus, foreshadows the lovers' leap at the end of *Smith* when she declares that death is a way of preserving perfect felicity.[21] The escape from life through suicide (or a more conventional death) is in fact more than an escape for Davidson: it represents also a triumph over circumstances. Life may bear down hard on the lover or the artist, but he has a trump card to play that will take the last trick. When he wishes, he can take his own life, cheating fate of its final victory.[22] In *Romantic Farce* and *Bruce*, Davidson believes man is able to control circumstances and defy fate, although *Smith* indicates a fuller awareness of the difficulty of doing so.

In *Smith*, Davidson is deeply concerned with the artist's search for recognition. Although he had not in 1886 given up teaching for a full-time career as a writer, he had had two works published, *The North Wall* and *Diabolus Amans*, and had no doubt felt the chagrin of seeing his works ignored or neglected. However, Davidson's attitude toward the artist is again ambiguous; the irony of a farcical tragedy hangs over the play. Hallowes has a convincing enough dedication to the high cause of art, but he expires almost ludicrously while mouthing a two-page soliloquy. Smith is speaking in Davidson's style when he recommends smiting a passage through the close-grained world, but his melodramatic plunge off the cliff in the very last moment of the play has overtones of sheer ridiculousness. There is a strong note of despair, but there is undoubtedly a note of detachment toward the Byronic posturings of the two heroes. Many touches of humor which I have not indicated in my quotations substantiate this argument. Davidson is beginning to realize that the quest for fame may be much harder than he had expected and that mastering circumstances may require more courage than he has.

Also in Smith and Hallowes both poet and thinker are portrayed, and both are projections of the author. Very seldom are poet and thinker separated in Davidson's works. Only in a few of his lyrics and in some of his fiction of the 1890's is the propagator of ideas suppressed in favor of the entertainer or craftsman. The coupling of the poet and the thinker in *Smith* is a symbolic joining together which Davidson only occasionally put asunder in the years to follow.

I do not mean to imply, however, that Davidson's art with a message was always work of high seriousness and gravity. *Scaramouch in Naxos: a Pantomime,* written in 1888,[23] is chiefly a comic satire on the business ethics of the theater; but it also seriously sets forth some of Davidson's ideas about love. While the play is fairly successful, and was Davidson's favorite among his early plays, the topical satiric message need not concern us much. Scaramouch, an English impresario, visits Naxos in order to try to capture Bacchus, with whom he hopes to entertain his tasteless audiences back home. Davidson makes amply clear that he has a rather low opinion of both theater audiences and theater management.

The subplot is more important to a study of Davidson's ideas. Ione, a mortal living in Naxos, falls in love with a god, just descended to earth, who she thinks might be Endymion. She does not know who he is because he cannot talk until Bacchus arrives on the scene and loosens his tongue with some ambrosial wine. He is Sarmion, an inhabitant of some unnamed star. Sarmion has his choice of returning to the heavens and a purely spiritual existence, or loving the human Ione and living the life of a mortal. Like Browning's hero in "The Last Ride Together," Sarmion chooses mortal love, thereby rejecting an immortal spiritual existence for a life of human love with Ione. But, as we have noted in *Diabolus Amans,* love is immortal; hence, according to Davidson, lovers have immortality. Plainly, immortality gained through the medium of physical love and death is preferable to the purely spiritual state which Sarmion enjoyed on his star.

Thus, in *Scaramouch* Davidson re-emphasizes his belief in what I have called "supernatural naturalism"; that is, he believes in a spiritual world which is approached through the material. In our universe, the "spirit must be draped in mortal flesh," but nonetheless Sarmion and Ione will find through the fleshly union of love a richer existence. Like Davidson, they discover a personal God through their own emotional experiences.

## VI  *Summary of the Early Works*

Looking back over the works discussed so far, it becomes clear that rejection of authority and wrestling with spiritual problems are important themes in the early works, as in all of Davidson. His religious questioning places him in the tradition of the great nineteenth-century writers, both Romantics and Victorians. Undoubtedly, of greatest importance to Davidson is Carlyle; but the scientific viewpoint, as expressed by Darwin, Spencer, and Huxley, must also have influenced him.

The authority centered in the Bible or in the theological deductions from it—anything, in short, which is based on divine revelation—is the first to be rejected. Though the rejection of theological systems implies a rejection of the ethical systems attached to those theologies, and though Davidson attacks "fashion, propriety, convention" in general, he is not yet prepared to repudiate conventional morality fully. This situation is evident from his satiric treatment of the amoral novelist in *The North Wall* and also in Angelus' confession of guilt in *Diabolus Amans*.

Also, there is a deep current of ambiguity in Davidson's early works: he rejects fashions, propriety, conventions; yet he is concerned about the sins of his youth. His hero the courtier in *A Romantic Farce* tells his friends to master circumstances, but the hero of *The North Wall* who actually sets out to do so is treated satirically. As I have shown, an attitude of ironic detachment is responsible for the ambiguity. In calling all authority into question, Davidson also questions the validity of his own experiences and his personal beliefs. The result is an ironic ability to believe and to question at the same time, or, to put it differently, to be committed and detached about one and the same thing. Davidson's romantic irony thus colors anything we say about his ideas, especially in the works written after about 1884; nevertheless I think we may correctly argue that Davidson is more committed than detached. Even though he makes fun of his novelist-hero and treats somewhat farcically the suicides of his two heroes in *Smith,* the underlying convictions are plain enough. Reading Davidson convinces us that he held his beliefs strongly in spite of himself, for the irony is seldom fully convincing. The statement of belief (or disbelief) invariably carries more conviction than the ironical questioning of it. This irony, however, continues in the works of his middle period, where it becomes more pervasive and is better sustained.

# CHAPTER 3

## *Ironic Detachment: 1890-1900*

> "The poet, I understand, must not condemn, must not blame."
> "That is the ultimate fate of the poet, I believe. A thoroughly awakened intelligence dare not despise anybody or anything."
> —John Davidson, "Tête-àTête," 1898

THE decade from 1890 through 1900 was the most fruitful time of Davidson's career. His writings are numerous, the themes many and varied, the forms widely ranging. He wrote or published 5 volumes of poetry, 4 novels, 3 books of short stories, 164 known items in periodicals (reviews, critical essays, travel narratives, fiction, poetry), besides writing 4 original plays and making English adaptations of at least 3 foreign plays.. During these years Davidson first knew the joys of success, even of a certain amount of fame, and enough notoriety to have a poem parodied.[1] He had personal friendships with most of the figures of the London literary and publishing world.

In this wide range of materials available for the study of this period, there is a high degree of homogeneity in the ideas expressed. In fact, this homogeneity leads me to consider the 1890's as a definite "period" in Davidson's development, for his philosophic position in 1900 was in most essentials that of 1890. Davidson's ideas during these years may be grouped around two central themes, which run through all of his works. First, Davidson continues to protest against creeds, as he did in the early works, though in the 1890's the protest includes all externally imposed value systems—literary, scientific, social, ethical. His world view is completely colored by a kind of detachment which he calls simply "irony." But, in spite of the ironic point of view, Davidson is still worried about the riddles of the universe—God, the soul,

the nature of reality. Thus, one of the centers around which Davidson's ideas group themselves is the problem of the relationship
between irony and belief.

The second of the centers, which is partly in opposition to the
other, includes Davidson's ideas about heroes and hero worship.
Though his ironic detachment at this time leads him to question
to a certain extent the efficacy of heroic behavior, there are in any
case many portraits of the hero, some ironic, some serious. In some
of the later writings of this decade, Davidson abandons his ironic
detachment in this particular area of his thought to express a philosophy of "might means right" and to jingoism and racial pride.

Though sometimes these two sets of ideas, irony and heroism,
are closely interrelated, even presented side by side in one poem
(as in the eclogue "St. George's Day"), I will treat them in separate chapters in order to keep my analysis as clear as possible and
attempt to explain the relationships between them at the end of
the next chapter.

I  *"No creed for me": The Creed of Irony*

"A Ballad in Blank Verse of the Making of a Poet" is Davidson's
most important autobiographical statement of the period.[2] In this
poem he leaves us a record, essentially correct in psychological
details, of his break with Evangelicalism, his rejection of creeds
and his subsequent assumption of a creed of "no-creed," his "Everlasting No," and his "Center of Indifference."

Davidson, who casts himself as a boy growing up in Scotland,
loves Scotland; it "is world enough for me" (9). But there is one
serious problem: Scotland is the place where

> Time stands still
> And Change holds holiday; where Old and New
> Welter upon the border of the world,
> And savage creeds can kill.
>
> (29–30)

The boy's parents insist upon forcing him into the mold of their
narrow Evangelical Christianity. After a painful rejection of Evangelicalism, which the boy had first professed, even going so far as
to take communion, he goes to his father and explains the idea
which he has evolved to replace the God he rejected:

> Henceforth I shall be God; for consciousness
> Is God: I suffer; I am God: this Self,
> That all the universe combines to quell,
> Is greater than the universe; and *I*
> Am that I am. To think and not be God?—
> It cannot be! Lo! I shall spread this news,
> And gather to myself a band of Gods—
> An army, and go forth against the world,
> Conquering and to conquer.
>
> (22)

We cannot help but note how strikingly this passage seems to echo both the egotism and the language of Nietzsche in *Thus Spake Zarathustra*, in, for example, the section entitled "Of Higher Man" in the fourth and last part.[3] But, before jumping to any conclusions about the influence of Nietzsche, we must take account of certain factual and bibliographic data which help determine the extent of Nietzsche's influence on Davidson during the 1890's.

The "Ballad in Blank Verse" was published in *Ballads and Songs* in November, 1894. By 1894, Davidson was at least superficially acquainted with Nietzsche, for he had published an article in *The Speaker* for November 28, 1891, entitled "The New Sophist," in which he translated parts of an article about Nietzsche from a French journal. The French article, "Littérature Étrangère: Frédéric Nietsche, le dernier Métaphysicien," was the first of a series about current Continental writers by Theodor de Wyzewa, published in the *Revue Politique et Littéraire, Revue Bleue,* XLVIII (November 7, 1891).[4] Davidson's article is little more than a biographical account with about a column and a half of summary statements about Nietzsche's thought. These statements demonstrate two things: Davidson's ideas about Nietzsche were based at this time on no firsthand knowledge of Nietzsche's work; moreover, Davidson did not find Nietzsche particularly to his liking. "He is the Nihilist of philosophy," Davidson concludes in the *Speaker* essay. "After all, Nietzsche's Nihilism is little more than a recrudescence of *Sturm und Drang*. Goethe went through it, and came out serene; and Shakespeare did not turn mad after *Hamlet* and *King Lear,* but lived to write *The Tempest!*"

We must agree with John A. Lester, Jr., that, though this article seems to be the earliest published reference to Nietzsche in English, "Davidson was not fundamentally convinced or even fundamentally affected by Nietzsche in this first encounter." [5] Perhaps Davidson recognized in Nietzsche a kindred spirit, but the quotation clearly indicates that he had strong reservations about the value of the German philosopher's ideas. Nevertheless, Davidson retranslated the French article for a column, "Frederick Nietsche," which appeared in *The Glasgow Herald* for March 18, 1893.[6] And in *Sentences and Paragraphs* (1893), he reprinted some excerpts from the *Speaker* article (72–83). Thus, he did to some extent maintain his interest in Nietzsche.

An early translator and editor of Nietzsche, Oscar Levy, remarks that "it was in the year 1893 that Nietzsche's name is first mentioned in one of the books [*Sentences and Paragraphs*] of the unfortunate English poet John Davidson. In the following year a group of German, English, and Scottish admirers of Nietzsche arranged to bring out an authorized version of the German thinker's works, three volumes of which were actually published in 1896 and 1897." [7] Because Davidson did not read German,[8] we must conclude that his earliest thorough acquaintance with Nietzsche came with his reading of the English translations, or perhaps from the analysis of Nietzsche's thought by Havelock Ellis in three articles published in the *Savoy* in April, June, and August, 1896. Therefore, the apparent influence of Nietzsche on the poem in question, "Ballad in Blank Verse," or indeed on any writings up to April, 1896, must be discounted.

But, besides the echo of Nietzsche in "A Ballad in Blank Verse," there is a distinct suggestion of the proto-Romantic, perhaps one might say proto-Nietzschean, English poet, William Blake. In later years Davidson was familiar with Blake's writings;[9] and he may, through his contacts with W. B. Yeats and The Rhymers' Club during the 1890's, have come to know Blake's works well. In any case, the parallels between Blake, the early Romantic, and Davidson, the late Romantic, are striking. For example, the egoism of the persona in "A Ballad in Blank Verse" is remarkably similar to Blake as he speaks in, say, "The Marriage of Heaven and Hell." Both Blake and Davidson are iconoclastic, rebellious, anxious to reverse conventions, and unwilling to be bound by laws or creeds. In their protests against rules and regulations, both make intuition the standard against which the ethics of their actions are judged. Both discover an ironic, paradoxical universal, a reversal of the moral order in which good is evil and evil good, heaven is hell and hell heaven. Ultimately, both become prophets and system builders whose private cosmogonies are expressed in highly individual poetic idioms. And it is surely no coincidence that both felt they were fighting almost single-handedly against a corrupt or decaying moral order.

In the "Ballad in Blank Verse," the boy-poet's rejection of Christianity kills his father. The boy, reconsidering his impetuousness, decides that he has been a fool:

> "How unintelligent, how blind am I,
> How vain!" he said. "A God? a mole, a worm!
> ................................................................
> A God who said a little while ago,
> 'I'll have no creed;' and of his Godhead straight
> Patched up a creed unwittingly. . . ."
> (32–33)

Again he rejects religious creeds, the "ruthless creeds that bathe the earth in blood," but this time he refuses to replace the creed he is casting out (Christianity) with another (Man is God). Thus the boy arrives at his decision:

> *No creed for me!* I am a man apart:
> A mouthpiece for the creeds of all the world;
> A soulless life that angels may possess
> Or demons haunt, *wherein the foulest things*
> *May loll at ease beside the loveliest;*
> A martyr for all mundane moods to tear;
> The slave of every passion; and the slave
> Of heat and cold, of darkness and of light;
> A trembling lyre for every wind to sound.
> (34; italics mine)

The philosophic viewpoint expressed in the portions of the quotations which are italicized dominated Davidson's writing during the 1890's. Davidson himself called it "irony." Undoubtedly, its forerunner was the paradoxical ambiguity discussed in Chapter 2. The difference between the earlier irony and the irony that predominates in this later decade is that the latter is much more serious. The element of Byronic posturing which I associated with the early works is gone—recall Smith and Hallowes. Davidson no longer tries to conceal his sympathies; instead, he tries to get along without any sympathies at all. This irony has two effects on Davidson: on the one hand, he takes a position that is completely noncommittal ("no creeds for me"); on the other hand, he accepts the entire universe without question ("the foulest things . . . beside the loveliest"). Thus, the tendency present in Davidson from the very first, that tendency to reject all authority and conventions, his "everlasting no," has now become the basis for a whole philosophy of life, a sort of "center of indifference." Here, indeed, is a real basis for sympathy between Nietzsche and Davidson—the eternal questioning. Only toward the end of the 1890's does Davidson begin to leave this center of philosophic indifference—to move away from irony toward committal to a set of beliefs. However, Davidson's "everlasting yea" is found most fully in the works of his last years.

Documenting Davidson's ironic view of the world is largely a matter of selecting the best evidence. The first element, the rejection of all creeds, appears over and over again in the writings of the 1890's. Davidson states his position well in prose in *A Random Itinerary*, 1894.[10] In the person of the Itinerant, he tells of seeing a group of unemployed people in Hampton Court Home Park. He reasons to himself that the unemployed should perhaps be pressed into the military service; for, as he says, "no one could object to the compulsory enlistment of every able-bodied man who cannot find work" (77). However, he says, the Itinerant "would have pursued the question much further, but his terror of doctrinaires and people with fixed ideas is so great, that he banished the subject from his mind" (77).

An imaginative presentation of Davidson's terror of doctrinaires and people with fixed ideas is the poem, "A Woman and Her Son" (1897), in which a young man, emancipated, or who thinks he is, from the narrow Evangelicalism of his mother, returns to her deathbed to plead with her to renounce orthodox Christian beliefs about immortality. She dies believing but comes back to life again after three days, having found no heaven or hell; she dies the second time denying everything. Affected by this second death, the son goes mad, preaches that he is God, and says he will create a heaven for her. The conclusion of the poem reveals the theme:

> Thus did he see her harden with a hiss
> As life went out in the cold bath of death;
> Thus did she soften him before she died:
> For both were bigots—fateful souls that plague
> The gentle world.[11]

To Davidson, a "secular" creed may produce a bigot as well as a narrow religious creed.

## II  *Irony and the Religion of Science*

Davidson's fullest treatment of his terror of doctrinaires and bigots is the novel *Earl Lavender,* published in 1895. The book has a delightful title: *A Full and True Account of the Wonderful Mission of Earl Lavender, which Lasted One Night and One Day: with a History of the Pursuit of Earl Lavender and Lord Brumm by Mrs Scamler and Maud Emblem,* by John Davidson with a frontispiece by Aubrey Beardsley.[12] Earl Lavender is a man with a fixed idea. Evolution (always spelled with a capital "E") is his religion. As he explains it to Lord Brumm:

> ". . . I succeeded in thinking out for myself a sort of dogma of Evolution."
> "You may be said to have 'got Evolution' in this sudden way, just as people talk about 'getting religion.' "
> "Precisely. I was converted. Sometimes I can dogmatize about Evolution, and sometimes I can't; but since my conversion I have lived an evolutionary life—consciously, that is."
>
> (7–8)

The fantastic title and this quotation should make clear the satiric tone of this novel, as well as the chief target of the satire: Earl Lavender's dogmatism about Evolution. In a larger sense, Davidson is satirizing two tendencies: casting off traditional Christian belief only to become equally dogmatic about evolution, and applying Darwinism to problems of human relationships.

Earl Lavender himself illustrates both the foolishness of the doctrinaire and the ridiculousness of making a sociology of Darwinism. Earl Lavender tells Lord Brumm, his partner in evolutionary ventures, that he suspects that he is *"the fittest"*; indeed, he is "not among the fittest only, but *the* very fittest human male at present breathing" (8). Earl Lavender has two purposes in life: the first is to become "the active agent, the apostle of Evolution"

(9); the second, he says, is "to find the fittest woman, and mate with her. This is a more complicated matter than you may think. It may seem to you a very simple thing to give the world proof of my supreme fitness, and then advertise in *The Times* for the fittest woman. It is really a simple plan, and might be very successful" (10). It turns out that there are two important objections to the plan: Earl Lavender is broke, and he is already married—to the Maud Emblem of the title. Neither Earl Lavender nor Lord Brumm has any money; but, united by their respective desires to escape from Maud and Mrs. Scamler, they set off to conquer the world for Evolution, trusting to Evolution to provide for them. Like the disciples in Mark 6:8, they have no script, no bread, and no money in their purses.

The many religious parallels and allusions in *Earl Lavender* reinforce the satire upon evolution as a religion. The careers of Earl Lavender and Lord Brumm are similar in many instances to the careers of Jesus and his disciples, or to Saint Paul and his missionary assistants. For example, like Paul, Lavender experiences a sudden conversion; for, as we have already noted, he tells Lord Brumm that he "got Evolution" through some sort of divine revelation. He is a fervent enough follower of his new religion to be able to persuade Brumm to be his pupil; "You shall be my first disciple," Earl Lavender tells him. "We go forth tonight to conquer the world for Evolution" (15). Thus Lavender and Brumm, master and disciple, go forth into the world to preach the gospel to every creature.

Like Saul, who became known as Paul when he assumed leadership on his first missionary journey, the apostles of evolution take names suggestive of their offices, Earl Lavender comes from "Earl *de l'Avenir*": "As *l'avenir* [future] is wrapped up and concealed in my new name of Lavender, so the future is wrapped up in me" (18), he explains to Brumm. Lord Brumm's name indicates the part he is to play as a sweeper away of old creeds, "Mr. New Broom" (19).

As we have already noted, Lavender and Brumm set out to convert the world; but Lord Brumm is at times a reluctant follower, a man of little faith. Their method of bringing the world into the camp of the religion of evolution is to combine precept with example. Earl Lavender would demonstrate the precepts of the evolutionary life by simultaneously proclaiming them and testing them publicly. He hopes thus to create a mythology, or a gospel. As he explains to Lord Brumm, they will begin testing the power of evolution by going to a good restaurant and ordering a hearty meal, though they have no money to pay for it.

Thus, Lavender and Brumm make their way from one restaurant and club to another, testing the efficacy of Earl Lavender's gospel. Like Jesus Christ and his disciples, Lavender and Brumm even perform miracles, evolutionary miracles. As Earl Lavender says, "Take example by me. Not in parliaments, or cathedrals, or colleges, but in taverns and restaurants is the new doctrine preached; and its veracity is attested not by banners and trumpets and embattled hosts, but by a simple miracle which lay to my hand—to wit, the being publicly provided for at the expense of others—that is, by Evolution" (117).

During the third successful demonstration of evolution's ability to take care of its own, Earl Lavender and Lord Brumm meet a Veiled Lady who pays for their dinner (114). She conveys them at her expense to Trallidge's Hotel, which has a very dubious reputation; and there follows an extraordinary adventure which may be taken as a kind of harrowing of Hell, with the Veiled Lady as She-Devil. The missionaries discover that they have entered the "Underground City" populated by a society of Flagellants. Earl Lavender tries to preach his gospel there, and he also attempts to court the Veiled Lady, who he believes is the "fittest woman" for whom he is seeking. However, she quickly stops him with the cold statement that "there is no marriage, nor giving in marriage here" (132). Not to be so easily put down, Earl Lavender continues to protest his love for the Veiled Lady as well as to proclaim the gospel. As a result, he is called before the judgment seat, where he is judged by a white-robed sage who sentences him to be expelled from the Underground City (143). Though the biblical parallels are suddenly inverted, the suggestion of the final judgment before the great white throne is apparent.

On a second missionary journey into the Underground City, Earl Lavender states his message to the sage himself:

All the old creeds must be torn out though the heart of the world come with them. All art, all literature must begin over again. Religion must cease absolutely, and be for ever forgotten. Mark you, I do not mean only Christianity or religiosity, but I mean religion in the broadest sense in which the most advanced thinker may cling to it. For religion we must substitute Evolution. . . . Be converted; become an Evolutionist, and aid me in the conversion of all who visit these abodes.

(281)

The sage, the Nameless One, passes judgment on Earl Lavender by turning on him the cold light of common sense. "You must go marry," he tells him; "know the world; and endeavour to live a decent, honest life. You are only an exaggerated type in these latter days of individualism—fantastic creatures, made what they are by pseudo-philosophy, feeble poetry, and foolish fiction. Go; be human; and give nature a chance" (282). Earl Lavender is persuaded, and he is reconverted back into Sir Harry Emblem. He returns to Maud and to the realms of good sense, and he intends to follow the sage's advice to "marry and have children, read as your tastes direct you, and take a share in the world's work" (286).

Thus, the religious patterns in the novel support the satire on those who take evolution as their religion, and who forget that it is at best a working hypothesis. Earl Lavender is converted, gathers disciples, preaches, performs miracles, faces temptations, even descends into hell; but he finally sees the light and turns to a common-sense view of reality.

As they promulgate the religion of evolution, Earl Lavender and Lord Brumm are led on a wild chase in a stolen cab into Epping Forest where Earl Lavender discovers the "missing link." By poking fun at the jargon of the Darwinists, their distinguishing phrases such as "the survival of the fittest," "natural selection," and "the missing link," Davidson attacks the application of evolutionary theory to human relationships. As I have already noted, Earl Lavender says he is the fittest of all men to survive; therefore, he believes that he should mate with the fittest of women. He thinks he has found her in the Veiled Lady, but we learn later, though Lavender never does, that she is a "new woman" who will have nothing to do with the mundane business of marriage and childbearing. She suppresses her sexual desires by flagellation.

As Earl Lavender explains it to his wife Maud when she catches him in Epping Forest, he has a system for finding the fittest mate. He will entertain delegations from all nations of the world, choosing about a hundred of the best-favored women, and he will live a week with each in order to find the fittest mate. "Here it seems to me," he says to Maud, "you have a very fair scheme of Natural Selection" (239–40). Without a doubt, Davidson intends a very fair joke on Darwinists.

On their adventurous route to Epping Forest, Earl Lavender and Lord Brumm hear an extraordinary sound and discover a preposterous creature, "some compound monster it seemed—a double jinn or deeve sweetening its solitude with music" (190). Earl Lavender, who surveys the creature for five minutes, concludes that it is "the missing link." "It is now demonstrated," he says, "by our discovery of this double creature on the very first morning of the new era that the effort of Nature in evolving man from the lower animals produced a bi-formed beast, one portion of which became the progenitor of the human race, the other of the monkey tribe" (192–93). Even when Lavender learns that his "missing link" is a Scotch itinerant poet in kilts who is being set upon by an escaped circus orangoutan which got curious about the Scotchman's bagpipes, he insists that they must constitute the missing link. Only an "Evolutionary miracle" could have brought about such a juxtaposition, he says (202–3). Partly, of course, this incident is an elaborate piece of irony in which Davidson is joking about his own Scotch background, but more importantly, Davidson is suggesting that common sense should prevent a man from such vanity of dogmatizing.

*Earl Lavender* is surely no great book, but it contains some of the best of Davidson in it. The tone of irony is sustained very well, and the book exposes fashions as disparate as flagellation and Darwinian sociology with delightful common sense. There is an aura of Scotch sturdiness about the book: no nonsense and no effeteness with, at the same time, a healthy respect for quite ruggedly individualistic characters. The style is plain, clear, and manly, and the story is told straightforwardly and efficiently.

The structure of the book is episodic, almost picaresque; this occurs no doubt because the hero's quest is undertaken to prove that evolutionary purposes are fulfilled if he takes advantage of whatever circumstances he finds himself in. Thus, the episodic structure is functional and is, in fact, the only kind of structure possible.

The whole novel satirizes the application of Darwinism and its slogans to social problems, and such an application was the hallmark of Herbert Spencer's *Principles of Sociology* (1876–96).

R. M. Metz, a historian of British philosophy, says that Spencer's aim was "to show that social development is a phase of the universal evolutionary process. . . . Here, as elsewhere, in the system [his *System of Philosophy*], the Darwinian principle of selection is emphasized. It was Spencer, by the way, who matched the slogan 'the struggle for existence' with the equally famous one 'the survival of the fittest.' The Darwinian law of animal life was thus brought back by Spencer to the sphere of human life which, through Malthus, had first suggested it." [13]

Davidson did not want evolutionary theory applied to literature, and in a letter to Edmund Gosse, written on October 28, 1898, Davidson explains why:

. . . The evolutionary idea is even more misleading in Literature than in Science and Philosophy. Since the Ptolemaic system nothing more satisfactory to common sense has been offered in any branch of knowledge than Evolution; but it is now supposed that the sun does not go round the earth, and it may very well be that the apparent descent of Man is a sense-illusion too. I suggest that English literature is a forest rather than a plantation; that Evolution, applied to literature, reverses the proverb, and cannot see the trees for the wood; and that generalization, admirable for classes, is mischievous in dealing with individuals. I mean that we—that you and *I*, poets, thinkers, sinners, fortunate-unfortunates, authentic persons, or whatever we may call ourselves, or be called, *must accept no creed;* that although Evolution is bound to rule the minds of men for hundreds of years to come, the sinner—let us use sinner; it is a modest term—the sinner knows it will be dismissed in turn as Creation is being dismissed now; and that although he may be compelled to use the idea of Evolution in order to be understood of his contemporaries, he is unfettered by it, and rejoices in his liberty.[14]

This letter, and especially the final phrases and the italicized passage, indicate clearly that John Davidson was still apparently maintaining near the end of 1898 his ironic detachment toward dogma, no matter of what kind. He may use the terminology of evolution, he says, but he will not be bound by any one point of view—except the ironic.

### III  *Irony and Social Criticism*

In view of Davidson's intellectual detachment, it is somewhat surprising that he also became a social critic during the 1890's. A

writer who denies that there are any absolutes is also by implication denying that there are standards of judgment. If Davidson
has no standards, how can he set himself up as a social critic?
Against what norm does he measure society in order to criticize it?
Davidson does not answer this question, but there are at least two
implicit answers. The first may be found in *Earl Lavender;* the
standard against which Earl Lavender and his philosophy are
measured is the one that we might call "enlightened common
sense." Earl Lavender is finally dissuaded from his apostolic mission by what Davidson calls "quiet ridicule, and the dreadful
common-sense point of view." [15] Thus the uncommitted ironist
may take a certain pragmatic stand against what the *consensus
gentium* would agree is social injustice. Furthermore, though
Davidson is a social critic, he hesitates to supply solutions to the
social problems which he discussed, and he thereby preserves a
measure of detachment.

For example, one of Davidson's best-known poems, "Thirty Bob
a Week," [16] which T. S. Eliot says has given him inspiration, is a
poem of social criticism. The thirty-bob-a-week clerk, "a-scheming
how to count ten bob a pound" (92), reflects that

> P'r'aps we are in Hell for all that I can tell,
> And lost and damn'd and served up hot to God.
>
> I ain't blaspheming, Mr. Silver-tongue;
>     I'm saying things a bit beyond your art:
> Of all the rummy starts you ever sprung,
>     Thirty bob a week's the rummiest start!
> With your science and your books and your
>     the'ries about spooks,
>     Did you ever hear of looking in your heart?
>
> I didn't mean your pocket, Mr., no:
>     I mean that having children and a wife,
> With thirty bob on which to come and go,
>     Isn't dancing to the tabor and the fife:
> When it doesn't make you drink, by Heaven! it
>     makes you think,
>     And notice curious items about life.
>
>                                      (93–94)

Davidson's attitude toward the economic situation in 1894 is clear
enough: he does not like it. However, the approach is typically

ironic. There is no party line; the poem does not betray a Marxist, a Fabian Socialist, or a Christian bias. Davidson has no easy solution to offer, no partisan panacea to propose; but he recognizes that something is wrong when a man cannot make ends meet, and that is the point of the poem. Thus, the ironist maintains his detachment by recording his protest through the persona of an aroused, rather talkative, underpaid clerk.

### IV  *Irony and the Artist*

Davidson's distrust of creeds and systems extends to his thinking about literature and to his role as a writer. The artist must be free of restraints, whether in subject matter or in technique:

> No creed for me! I am a man apart:
> A mouthpiece for the creeds of all the world;
> ...............................................................
> A trembling lyre for every wind to sound,

is the way Davidson expressed his view poetically. If the artist hears the lark and linnet, he will sing of them. If he hears the cries of the workman's hungry children, he will write of them; if he hears both, he will write of both. No matter what the writer finds the world to be, he must be free to express himself. In one of the imaginary conversations which Davidson called "tête-à-têtes," Davidson and one John Smith say that it is not enough to call poetry, as Arnold had, a "criticism of life"; more than that, Davidson says,

Literature is a Statement of the World . . . and Poetry, being the inmost heart of Literature, might be called an Interpretation of the World. . . .
J.S. The poet, I understand, must not condemn, must not blame.
J.D. That is the ultimate fate of the poet, I believe. A thoroughly awakened intelligence dare not despise anybody or anything.[17]

The writer's freedom must be such that he may embrace everything. Poetry, Davidson writes, "is the most empirical of all the arts; in a sense every poet is a charlatan; he can give no authority except his own experience, his own imagination; in the last resort he can give no authority at all; he cannot tell; it was the Muse. Whether he be artificer or artist . . . it is liberty of utterance he seeks." [18] In thus seeking to expand the range of poetic subject matter, Davidson allies himself with many other poets and critics of the 1890's, especially Henley and Arthur Symons, the latter one of Davidson's fellow Rhymers.

The poet, Davidson continues, must remain ironically aloof in order to present reality as he sees it from his detached point of view, colored by his imagination and experience. Only so long as he retains this freedom will he be a successful artist. "The poet, the artist," Davidson writes, "will apply any creed, philosophy, system of morality or immorality to life, and wring the utmost terror and beauty from its action; but when he becomes the irredeemable victim of a philosophy or a creed it is all over with his poetry and art." [19] Yet clearly Davidson aligns himself with the critical traditions of English Romanticism, especially with Wordsworth's Preface to *Lyrical Ballads*. He depends on an overflow of powerful feelings; he wishes to create his own forms to express them in; he believes poetry can synthesize all knowledge; and he asks for criticism based on human experience instead of on rules.

In spite of Davidson's high ideal of the absolute demand on the writer to record experience as he finds it, Davidson is not sure that literature accomplishes anything. As we might expect, he approaches the subject of the artist's ability to change the world with his usual detachment. According to the autobiographical "Ballad in Blank Verse," he hoped through his ironic art to be "a trembling lyre for every wind to sound." More than that, irony would help him to be a spokesman for any and all, small and great, good and evil; and, therefore, he would be able to reign

> Prince of the powers of the air, lord of the world
> And master of the sea. Within my heart
> I'll gather all the universe, and sing
> As sweetly as the spheres; and I shall be
> The first of men to understand himself.[20]

Now that is a rather high ideal—prince of the powers of the air, lord of the world, and master of the sea, besides being the first man to understand himself. Presumably he is to arrive at this exalted position through his poetry, and that clearly is to be controlled by his desire as an ironist to "state the world" with all its contradictions, free of all restraints, including creeds.

Yet Davidson is not always so optimistic about what art will accomplish. In fact, he says very little about it during this period, and what he says is rather ambiguous. Nevertheless, we can gather something from his fictional presentations of the problems. A tantalizingly ambiguous statement about the ability of the artist to effect changes in his environment is the story "Miss Armstrong's Circumstances," the title story of a volume of short stories published in 1896.[21] The story expresses Davidson's point of view as it was during the earlier part of the decade—that is, of course, strongly ironic. Miss Armstrong, who is "just nineteen," is writing an autobiographical novel.

Miss Armstrong declares herself an antideterminist, one who believes she has her fate in her own hands. The morning after this great declaration, into her schoolroom (she is a governess; Davidson was a teacher) walks William Somers, the older brother of her three pupils. Somers dismisses the children, saying that he has a holiday. He invites Miss Armstrong to come with him to enjoy his holiday, a "Bank holiday," at which point she criticizes him for being only "a circumstance," who dares take his holidays only when the banks allow him. After her tirade, she relents a little, and, though she will not go with him, she allows him to come with her on what she describes as her "first assault on circumstances" (11). She is an artist, remember, and this first assault consists of going to see her old music-master, Herr Herman Neunzehn, to ask him to look over her compositions and give her an introduction to a publisher. When Herr Neunzehn turns her down, she tries to summon courage by telling herself, "The battle has begun; here's a circumstance with a vengeance: don't give in" (17–18). But give in she must, though she does persuade Herr Neunzehn to introduce her to Mr. Dapper, a composer, who also rejects her music flatly, and she is forced to admit, "Deep down in my own heart, I knew I had made a mistake about myself" (28). Nevertheless, though she fails in her attack upon circumstances, she and William Somers fall in love during their holiday, and, as she says later, "a little circumstance for which William and I are responsible—I *have* helped to cause something"—is now the center of her attention (29).

I have described this story at some length because it is a parable in which Davidson sets forth his ideas about whether or not one has any control over his environment. Thus, by extension, he deals with the question of whether or not the artist can change the world around him by means of his art. Though the idea is treated humorously, Miss Armstrong, like the poet in "Ballad in Blank Verse," believes that she is the first person to understand herself. She thinks that she may assume either an active or passive role in life, and she believes that she can be active and change things, just as an explorer, an artist, a poet, or a prime minister does. She regards herself as one of those strong natures who would, as Davidson's poet says, reign prince of the power of the air, lord of the world, and master of the sea. Of course, she starts with lesser, almost insignificant things; but, as she says, "if paltry circumstances were not to be combated, how was I to challenge and overcome the great ones which hemmed me in on all sides?" (10–11). Miss Armstrong has an extremely high ideal of what she may accomplish, but we have also seen that she fails in her first assault upon circumstances—fails utterly—and even admits to herself that she has been sadly mistaken. Her consolation is that she now has a husband and a baby, not exactly the circumstances she expected to create, but nevertheless, she has done something to change the world around her.

The story poses a problem which is explored in many of the other stories in the volume: "A Would-Be Londoner," "Alison Hepburn's Exploit," and "Among the Anarchists" are some of the pieces in the volume which explore man's ability to change circumstances—to assume an active role in controlling his own life as well as the lives of others. The parallels between Miss Armstrong and John Davidson are unmistakable. She is a natural mask for him: both are writers, both are teachers, both want to master themselves and the rest of the world—and both discover that mastering the world is not as easy as it appears to be. Thus, though the story concludes ambiguously, the point is clear: Davidson as usual is highly skeptical; he does not know whether one can control circumstances or not; he does not know whether the artist can affect life outside of the imaginary world that he creates in his writings. It seems finally that Davidson thinks the artist can accomplish little in the way of changing reality in the everyday world.

In one of his tête-à-têtes Davidson says, in a wry Carlylean statement, "People can't help themselves; they have language, they have pens and paper; one writes, another writes. And it is all inferior, the very highest of it, to a thing done. The power of the pen has been grossly exaggerated. Napoleon, not Goethe, made the modern world." [22] Nevertheless, Davidson continued writing on. He makes a partial explanation in the essay from which I have just quoted: "A poet is always a man of inordinate ambition and inordinate vanity." [23] Davidson still probably wanted to be the prince of the power of the air, lord of the earth, and master of the sea. Being a successful writer was one way to do it. But ironist that he was, he fully realized the difficulties involved.

### V  *"The foulest things besides the loveliest":*  *Irony and the Universe*

As we have seen, Davidson's rejection of systems during the decade of the 1890's extended beyond religion to a general "terror of doctrinaires and people with fixed ideas." He refused to accept evolution, Darwinism, Spencerian sociology, any system of political or economic reform, even any rules or restraint in his art. But another side of Davidson's irony remains to be discussed, the ability to accept the universe as he finds it, to allow "the foulest things to loll at ease beside the loveliest." It is something like what Keats called "negative capability," and it is very similar to the paradoxical reversal of good and evil that we see in Blake's "Marriage of Heaven and Hell." Davidson simply calls it "irony." It complements the ironist's apparent rejection of all standards of judgment; it involves the acceptance of all things. Davidson's eclogue, "St. Valentine's Eve," written in 1893 illustrates this.[24] As Menzies complains to Percy of the wretchedness of his life as an aspiring writer, Percy, who is an ironist, explains that he looks upon "All the blight/ Of pain, age, madness, ravished innocence,/ Despair and impotence" as the other part of love, indeed, "Love's needful shadow" (24). Existence requires that we willingly accept both the poles, love and despair, pleasure and pain: "The groaning of a universe in pain/ Were as an undersong in Love's refrain" (25).

Percy's point of view, which is repeatedly expressed in the eclogues, is stated by Davidson himself in a series of letters to the editor of the *Speaker* in March, April, and May of 1899. The exchange, which at first was between Davidson and A. T. Quiller-Couch, discussed the proper subject matter of poetry. Davidson, in defending his point of view, argued for an all-embracing irony:

"I love *Irony*; and I would rather be than not be. . . . Poetry itself
. . . represents the *Irony* which is the soul of things, and of which
what are called Good and Evil, Beauty and Ugliness, are attributes." [25] In another letter Davidson explains that irony is for him
a complete explanation of the universe, not just a poetic view of
the universe: "Worshipful Irony," he writes, "the profound 'Irony
of fate,' is doubtless responsible for Renanism, and all 'isms, but is
derived from none of them. It is centric, the adamantine axis of
the universe. At its poles are the illusions we call matter and spirit,
day and night, pleasure and pain, beauty and ugliness. . . . Irony
is the enigma within the enigma, the open secret, the only known
answer vouchsafed the eternal riddle." [26] The universe is a paradox.

The final word of Davidson's series of letters on the subject of
irony summarizes his philosophic position:

I am not a Mocker; Mockery and Irony are not synonyms, as I understand them. . . .
My concern is not exclusively with "the best, the noblest, and the
happiest," but with the universe as I can grasp it. Irony is not a creed.
The makers of creeds have always miscalled, denied some part of the
world. Irony affirms and delights in the whole. Consciously, it is the
deep complacence which contemplates with unalloyed satisfaction Love
and Hate, the tiger and the nightingale, the horse and the blow-fly,
Messalina and Galahad, the village natural and Napoleon. Unconsciously, it is the soul of the Universe. Steep Irony in chaos, and the
universe will string itself about it like crystals on a thread. Whence
comes Chaos? Whence comes Irony? There is no reply. To believe that
the universe was *made* is the essence of anthropomorphism. I would
have no more interest in a made universe than in an eight-day clock or
a suburban villa. Thought cannot conceive, nor fancy call by any name,
the manner and agency of the becoming of the universe. But I perceive
the universe as a golden bough of Irony, flowering with suns and
systems.[27]

Irony is two things: it is Davidson's view of the world, and it is
the nature of the universe itself. Thus, irony is not only a way of
accepting life as he finds it with all its contradictions, but these
very contradictions describe the universe. The universe is amoral;
it is not bound by systems which man may try to impose upon it
or judge it by. Irony is "the soul of things," on the one hand; on

the other, it is Davidson's attitude toward the "enigma within the enigma." If irony affirms and delights in the whole, so does Davidson the ironist.

## VI  *Irony and Nature*

Because Davidson willingly takes the universe as he finds it, he is a sort of "naturalist," if we may use that word to denote someone who advocates the acceptance of all things natural. In a Wordsworthian sense, Davidson wishes to be "in harmony with nature." Davidson's ideas about nature may be best explained by citing several of the poems of the nineties, one of them the somewhat famous and frequently anthologized "Ballad of a Nun."[28] In this poem, we find an ironic inversion of orthodox morality into Davidsonian naturalism. A kind of tract, the poem urges the acceptance of the goodness of natural desires and the rightness of uninhibited self-expression. The protagonist of the ballad, the nun, whom her abbess trusts enough to have appointed doorkeeper, finds herself aroused by her natural desires, or, as we would say in contemporary idiom, by her sex drives. Though she scourges herself, she still has the "same red sin to purge":

> For still night's starry scroll unfurled,
> And still the day came like a flood:
> It was the greatness of the world
> That made her long to use her blood.
>
> (54)

That golden bough of irony, the universe, as Davidson says, calls to the nun to accept it and her clearly sexual passion as right because it is natural. The nun, sounding a bit like Swinburne, declares her intentions:

> Life's dearest meaning I shall probe;
> Lo! I shall taste of love at last!
> ...................................................
> I leave the righteous God behind;
> To go to worship sinful man.
>
> (56)

Leaving the convent, the nun arrives in the city and wastes no time trying out her nature; she gives herself to a "grave youth nobly dressed":

[ 56 ]

He healed her bosom with a kiss;
She gave him all her passion's hoard;
And sobbed and murmured ever, "This
Is life's great meaning, dear, my lord."

"I care not for my broken vow;
Though God should come in thunder soon,
I'm sister to the mountains now,
And sister to the sun and moon."

(57)

Like the ironist Davidson, the nun is completely in harmony with nature. By following the lead of her most powerful drives (and most "natural," Davidson would say), she has achieved a kind of fulfillment which makes her sister to the earth (the mountains) and to the whole universe (the sun and moon). Accepting what is natural without making a judgment about whether it is right or wrong has even brought her to the point of sisterhood with the Virgin Mary. For when the nun returns to the convent, she is prepared for the punishment of being buried alive. Instead, she is met by a new doorkeeper who lets her in, raises her tenderly from her knees, and asks whether the nun knows her; "Who art thou?" the nun asks. The new wardress answers:

"God sent me down to fill your place:
I am the Virgin Mary now."

And with the word, God's mother shone:
The wanderer whispered, "Mary, hail!"
The vision helped her to put on
Bracelet and fillet, ring and veil.

"You are sister to the mountains now,
And sister to the day and night;
Sister to God."

(61)

Davidson does not explain how Mary could be an advocate of his philosophic naturalism and still be a virgin; perhaps we are to assume that, like Davidson, she does not necessarily practice her theories.[29] But, in any case, naturalism has taken the place of orthodox Christianity in the poem; inasmuch as Davidson retains a Christian mythos, he inverts it so as to have God giving this stamp of approval to the actions of the nun which seem to reflect Davidson's personal philosophy. On the other hand, Davidson is by no means propagandizing for unrestrained sensuality or abandoned hedonism. Aside from the fact that Davidson was still too much of an Evangelical for that, his terror of doctrinaires and his ironic frame of mind would prevent him from making of the nun's naturalism a doctrine of hedonism to replace the asceticism which she freed herself from.

Davidson's position is clarified in a letter to Grant Richards about a proposed review of the poem in November, 1894. Davidson argues that we are not to think of the nun's experience as a bout of depraved sensuality, and he complains that the reviewer proposes to speak of unnatural crimes and nymphomania. The nun, he says, is not depraved: she is a healthy woman.[30] To Davidson, the nun is a healthy woman, for he often equates woman's healthiness with sexual fulfillment. This fulfillment means, not unrestrained sexual activity, but marriage and childbearing. For example, in Davidson's novel *Baptist Lake* (1896), the women in the Inglis family are all pregnant. Mr. Inglis tells Baptist Lake (the protagonist): "I like children, and I like mothering women, and I mean to have all my grandchildren born in my own house. The two girls you saw tonight—I could go down on my knees, and kiss their feet whenever I turn my eyes on them. To me a woman is sweetest looking when she is nearer her time—like a ripe fruit. To be fruitful is better than to be sterile, isn't it?" (124). At the end of *Baptist Lake*, the two girls mentioned in the quotation have had their babies; another Inglis daughter has had a baby; and Mrs. Inglis herself is pregnant, though she has several grandchildren. For Davidson, to be fruitful is to be "natural"; it is to accept the universe with all its contradictions—both the joys and the pains of childbirth and child rearing.

Davidson also uses the Tannhäuser legend to illustrate his ironic view of the universe. In a note to the poem, "A New Ballad of Tannhäuser," he makes this very clear: "The story of Tannhäuser is best known in the sophisticated version of Wagner's great opera. In reverting to a simpler form I have endeavoured to present passion rather than sentiment, and once more to bear a hand in laying the ghost of an unwholesome idea that still haunts the world—*the idea of the inherent impurity of nature*" (italics mine).[31] Clearly, Davidson is again using sexual passion as a

metaphor to refer to the idea of "naturalness." Sex is a function of
the body; the body is that portion of man which plainly relates
him to the rest of nature. Many thinkers and writers in the Western tradition have urged the suppression of the body, but Davidson portrays Tannhäuser's love for Venus as good. Unlike the
conventional legend, Davidson's retelling finds Tannhäuser completely happy in his naturalistic love. When Tannhäuser goes to
see Pope Urban, the pope makes his usual statement about the
blossoming of the dead staff; in the poem, the staff burst forth immediately, in the presence of all:

> The undivined, eternal God
> Looked on him from the highest heaven,
> And showed him by the budding rod
> There was no need to be forgiven.
>
> (109)

Tannhäuser leaves the Pope's presence to return joyfully to the
bosom of Venus.

Davidson wants to remind us again of his ironic philosophy:
"Irony affirms and delights in the whole." Natural impulses are
not evil, but they may instead be the promptings of God, as were
those of the nun and Tannhäuser. Davidson chooses sexual passions as his means for talking about "delight in the whole" no
doubt for several reasons. The rationalistic and scientific traditions of Western thought have long regarded thinking as man's
distinctive function. Similarly, the religious and intellectual worlds
have all too often denied the flesh; and they have done so as if
thinking were a function that takes place in an organism in spite of
its fleshliness instead of a function of that organism which cannot
be separated from all its other functions. Davidson is trying to
destroy the strong notion that a disembodied rationality is possible
and therefore to restore some kind of wholeness to man. He wishes
to affirm that sex is good, that the body is good, that the earth is
good.

Davidson thus squarely places himself in a line of writers whom
we now regard as modern prophets: Blake, who tries to "marry
heaven and hell" by showing us that our energies are healthy;
Nietzsche, who again and again attacks the denial of the flesh;
Freud, who suggests to us how central sex is to all phases of life;

D. H. Lawrence, who argues for the redemptive and healing powers of sexual expression. Although I do not want to try to make of Davidson a modern prophet, I do wish to call attention to the perceptiveness and relevance of his thought. The theme of the "Ballad of a Nun" and the "Ballad of Tannhäuser" has come to be one of the liberating ideas of recent times; and, whatever we may say about our contemporary obsession with sex, most of us would not be willing to trade it for Victorian suppression and prudery. In other words, we would say that Davidson is right.

Thus far in this chapter we have seen that Davidson's ironic point of view has two focuses. On the one hand, he refuses to commit himself to any one set of beliefs, be they religious or otherwise. On the other hand, he is willing to take things as they come, to accept the universe with all its contradictions. The paradox is that the universe itself is ironic in its very nature. Davidson tries to be in a very specific sense "in harmony with nature." This means accepting as natural, and therefore right, whatever impulses or intuitions one has. "Whatever is, is right" comes very close to describing Davidson's philosophy, even closer than it comes to Pope's. For Davidson refuses even to label evil as evil: a man who accepts everything cannot very well say that evil is good. Pope tried to explain how evil ultimately works for good; Davidson says there is no such things as evil. It is true, as Townsend says, that, for Davidson at this time, "sin and virtue are synonymous." [32]

VII  *"The Cat-Call of the Universe": Lingering Problems of Belief*

Nevertheless (and it is a big *nevertheless,* for I am about to contradict many things I have said), in spite of Davidson's protestations about his ironic detachment toward creeds and his refusal to accept any of them, the problem of belief remained with him. "It is in their attack that men reveal themselves," Davidson wrote; "the object of assault is always their own original sin. There is no more exalted quack than Carlyle; no more intolerant Philistine than Matthew Arnold." [33] And, to apply the same formula to the writer, there is a no more dogmatic doubter than John Davidson. The object of his assault was doctrine, or dogma, or any set of fixed ideas; his original sin was to want answers to all important questions—to have, in short, doctrine, dogma, and fixed ideas. As Kaufmann says in his *Nietzsche,* "It would seem to be a common psychological fact that man often craves religious certainty in direct proportion to his profound and tormenting doubtings." [34]

For a man of Davidson's nature, the ironic enigma of the universe demanded a solution. Seemingly, he could not quiet the old nagging questions about the nature of reality. In spite of all his talk about detachment and its apparent success in his own life (the 1890's were his most productive years), he was still in search of a belief. Though we could scarcely have ventured a guess in 1898 that he would say yes to scientific materialism, the abandonment of the ironic point of view, which occurred around 1901, should not have been much of a surprise.

Davidson describes his need for a belief with rather desperate humor in an article called "On the Downs," published in 1898:

When a Scotsman finds himself at cross-purposes with life, what course does he follow? He may say to himself, as the Itinerant [Davidson] did, "I will go and walk about the downs." Or he may say, "I will create a great poem"; or "I will go and preach in Hyde Park." He may say this, and he may say that, but he invariably does one of two things. He either sits down and drinks deeply, thoughtfully, systematically of the amber spirit of his country, or he reads philosophy. The Itinerant read philosophy. Doubtless, philosophers never read philosophy: they have no necessity to do so. The universe is as clear to them as a crystal ball, or a soap-bubble, or a whinstone—each according to his own theory. But to the ordinary layman and heavily-burdened wayfarer, above all to Scotsmen at cross purposes with life, philosophy is a sad temptation. To the very man in the street, indeed, it occasionally happens that the riddle of the universe grows vehement in its appeal; and, however secretly and shamefastly, "the poor inhabitant below" examines again the interpretations that have been wrought out by others; sets himself to answer the problem anew; finally burns his books, shaves, dines at a restaurant, and returns to Picadilly and the bosom of his family. [35]

Undoubtedly Davidson himself was in 1898 at cross-purposes with life and had been reading philosophy, and some of it was the philosophy of Friedrich Nietzsche. Earlier in this chapter, I showed that Davidson could not have read Nietzsche until the first English translations appeared in 1896 and 1897. *The Case of Wagner, Nietzsche contra Wagner, The Twilight of the Idols,* and *The Anti-Christ,* translated by Thomas Common, were published in one volume in the spring of 1896. *Thus Spake Zarathustra,* translated by Alexander Tille, followed in the same year; and in 1897 *A Genealogy of Morals* and *Poems* appeared in one volume, translated by W. A. Haussman and John Gray.

Davidson refers to these volumes in a letter to the editor of the *Daily Chronicle* for May 23, 1902: "A year or two ago I knew by heart the three published volumes of the English translations of Nietzsche, and found them as literature very admirable and exciting." John A. Lester, Jr., who has thoroughly examined the Nietzsche-Davidson relationship, suggests that Davidson learned Nietzsche "by heart" during the winters of 1896–97 and 1897–98, which he spent away from London in Shoreham, Sussex, on the English Channel coast, and from that time the Nietzschean influence is undeniable.[36] This conclusion would of course be substantiated by Davidson's statement quoted above, written in 1898, that he (the Itinerant) "read philosophy."

However, in the same letter to the editor quoted above, Davidson denies that he is Nietzsche's disciple; but that denial does not preclude the possibility of influence. He is perhaps following the advice of the protagonist of his novel, *Baptist Lake,* who says that one should never talk of "sources of knowledge. One's information is one's own, no matter where it came from, or however elementary it may be." [37] It is hard to imagine that he could be so interested in Nietzsche as to know his translated works "by heart" without being in a frame of mind to be influenced. In any case, as we noted before, Nietzsche's persistent questioning and his concern with the great riddles of existence must have struck a ready response in Davidson. What we must remember here is, as Lester says, that "Davidson found in Nietzsche a man who had heard as keenly as he the 'cat-call of the Sphinx.'" [38]

In the "Eclogue of the Downs," published in June, 1900,[39] Davidson shows that *he* has been at cross purposes with life; and *he* has probably been reading philosophy. One of the speakers in the eclogue, Lucian, is greatly concerned about the riddles of the universe:

> What and why:
> Conundrums all men ask, before the world,
> Or shamefaced and in secret.
>                                            (148)

Urban, another speaker (urbane, detached, Davidson the ironist?),
repeatedly tells him: "Of what and why? Nay, here and now"; but
the question continues to come up:

> Yes, but we cannot fling these questions off:
> They're in the blood, not fashionable wear,
> And drive the simplest and subtlest mad.
>
> (150)

On the edge of the downs the three speakers, Lucian, Urban, and
Eustace, find a run-down inn, the Fox and Hounds. Lucian, a
wanderer like the Itinerant in "On the Downs," has been there
before; and he recalls some one he once met there: "a savage oaf/
That skulked and tippled" (155), one who fits the description of
the Scotsman at cross purposes with life who drinks and philoso-
phizes. This fellow had done both, Lucian recalls:

>                        "Sir," says he,
> Waving his tankard, "did you ever hear
> The Cat-call of the Universe?"
> ............................................................
> "What do you mean by Cat-call?" "Don't you know?
> ............................................................
>                       Sphinx is now
> A symbol of the Universe; her call,
> The queries *what* and *why*. . . ."
>
> (153–54)

This same "savage oaf" appears in an article entitled "The Cat-Call
of the Sphinx," published in *The Star* (February 17, 1898). Davidson tells of meeting him in the Fox and Hounds—the "Other Customer," he calls him. The Other Customer explains how the Cat-
call comes: "For weeks, for months, it is silent, and then some
night suddenly in a theatre or a club, in the House of Commons,
or some other public-house, the Cat-call of the Sphinx pierces my
ear, and I forsake everything to have another try at the everlasting
conundrum."

Davidson wonders what the Other Customer means by the
Sphinx's riddle. It is not the riddle one finds in the Classics, he insists: "The Sphinx is now a symbol, and her cat-call is the question, 'What is the universe?' to some; 'Why is the universe?' to

others." The metaphor of a cat-call suggests the persistence with which the questions recur. "It seems to me difficult to express more vehemently the terrible obsession which the questions 'What' and 'Why' have in some moods than by just such a phrase as the cat-call of the Sphinx. . . . A time will come, sir, aye, and a time and a half, too, when you will hear that intolerable yell, and have nothing in the shape of missiles to reply with except a few stale antinomies. . . ."

The "savage oaf" and the "Other Customer" are not necessarily John Davidson, but these personae emphasize Davidson's great concern with the problem of "what and why." The poem is a dialogue of the mind with itself, as are all of Davidson's eclogues. The eclogue, of course, is readily adaptable to a kind of interior dialogue, because the eclogue traditionally involves more than one person and because a debate of some sort is often the purpose of the poem. Thus the eclogue is a natural form for the weighing of ideas. So both sides of Davidson find their expression: the Scotsman who worries about the riddle of the universe; the savage oaf who hides away in a frowzy inn on the downs and tries to shout down the cat-call of the universe; that part which cannot ignore the question of what and why, as well as the other side of Davidson, the ironist, who just a year before the "Eclogue of the Downs" was published was saying that "Irony is the enigma within the enigma, the open secret, the only answer vouchsafed the eternal riddle."

To a certain extent, the recurrence of an interest in the problems of belief shows a chronological development. Davidson began the decade with a terror of doctrinaires and of people with fixed ideas; but, by 1900, the old questions of doctrine and dogma were cropping up again, pointing to the commitment Davidson would make to a materialistic creed. Probably, the questions about spiritual matters were nagging him all the time.

## VII    *Presentiments of Materialism*

When William Archer inquired of Davidson in 1894 about the meaning of the conclusion of "A Ballad of a Nun," he explained first the naturalistic moral of the poem (see Townsend, 500–502, from which I quote): "Accepting the idea of God the import is that God's sympathies were entirely with the nun: the Virgin on withdrawing tells her that not only has she made herself one with

Nature by employing her body, however blindly, for its own appointed purpose, but has also made herself one with God while committing what she supposed to be deadly sin" (500).

Davidson then included a blasphemous, comic version of the poem, part of which is an ironic presentment of the materialism that was to come after 1900. In it, God is speaking to Christ and Mary: "It flabbergasts me quite! The intolerable mess these people make of every message given them. Look at all these lovely women and handsome fellows—made for each other!—shutting themselves up apart in order to save their souls. There again, now. Souls! What maggot has got into their heads I can't make out. I made them what they are—one and entire, and they go and divide themselves up into a trinity, and me too—mind, body, spirit. It's like my own grace, past finding out" (500). The tone is comic, but the idea seems to be plain enough: there is no spirit apart from the material. Nietzsche surely comes to mind at this point, for Zarathustra says in "Of the Despisers of the Body" that "the awakened, the enlightened man says: I am body entirely, and nothing beside; and soul is only a word for something in the body." [40] Davidson could have found the same thing in Blake, as I have already pointed out, but it is scarcely necessary to say Davidson used either one. All were, no doubt, kindred spirits.

The seeds of Davidson's final materialistic synthesis were present in the 1890's, in spite of the irony which kept him from becoming dogmatic about everything except irony. One poem in particular is a dramatic presentment of the philosophy of the later works and provides a convenient transition to the ideas of heroic vitalism which should be discussed before we turn to the final decade. Set in the years of Napoleon's victorious conquest of Europe, "The Vengeance of the Duchess," published in 1894,[41] tells of a Duchess who is celebrating her fifth wedding anniversary. She is reminded by it of Casimir, a man whom she banished to the mercury mines on her wedding day five years before because he had dared aspire to her hand. But Casimir is not beaten; somehow during his five years underground he has become a Davidsonian ironist and has learned to accept a seemingly evil universe. However, his universe is distinctly evolutionary. There is evidence that Davidson has been reading his Darwin and his Spencer, with some sympathy, in spite of the elaborate satires on Darwinism. "Nothing can touch my soul," says Casimir,

To discord with the universe. I understand the whole
Great wonder of creation: every atom in the earth
Aches to be man unconsciously, and every living birth—
The lowest struggling motion and the fiercest blood on fire,
The tree, the flower, are pressing towards a future ever higher,
To reach that mood august wherein we know and suffer pain.

(69–70)

Again the ideas are presented through a persona; Casimir, not Davidson, is speaking, and we are given to understand later in the poem that perhaps Casimir is mad. Yet Casimir is, like Davidson, an ironist, and he is treated with a great deal of sympathy. The seeds of Davidson's materialistic synthesis are present here: man is made of the same atoms as the lowest form of being; every atom is trying to become man; and man's nature might be described thus: "Man is matter become self-conscious." This last statement is a materialistic slogan which I have taken out of context from the writings of Davidson's final years, but it clearly fits Casimir's theory.

In this period, Davidson seems to have come full circle. He began the decade of the 1890's by rejecting all creeds, but the problems of belief never stopped troubling him. There was even a presentiment of the scientific (or pseudoscientific) slogans that became his creeds in 1901. But, before we discuss Davidson's movement toward the synthesis of heroic vitalism and materialism around which his thought centers in the final years, we must consider the development of his ideas about the hero—the subject of the next chapter.

# CHAPTER 4

# Hero Worship: 1890-1900

"Then I began to read Carlyle, and I have had no rest
since the day I opened *Heroes and Hero-Worship*."
—Ninian Jamieson, in Davidson's *Perfervid*

DURING the decade of the 1890's, Davidson said a great deal
about heroes and hero worship, as did many writers in the
Western world. Veneration of defiant, heroic natures is, of course,
by no means a purely nineteenth-century phenomenon: English
literature, indeed world literature, abounds in activist heroes.[1] But
perhaps because heroic vitalism contrasts so strongly with its
polar opposite during the 1890's, the so-called decadence or *fin-
de-siècle*, such vitalism, or the "counter-decadence" as Jerome
Hamilton Buckley calls it, seems almost a literary movement.[2]
Thus in writing about heroism, Davidson is not particularly original; for ideas of heroes and hero worship were everywhere. Henley, Rudyard Kipling, John Ruskin, Carlyle, Browning, and
Charles Kingsley are some of the English names we associate with
Victorian hero worship; and it is very hard to decide who may
have most strongly influenced Davidson. Browning, and certainly
Carlyle, are of first importance to Davidson; but their ideas were
so thoroughly a part of Victorian culture by the time he was
growing up that we can only say that Davidson shows many tendencies which call to mind Browning and Carlyle. Davidson had
written a good deal of "heroic" poetry and drama before Henley
had published "Invictus," and Nietzsche's writings, as we have
noted, did not appear in English translation until 1896 and 1897.[3]

## I  The Davidsonian Hero

In Chapter 2, I described a number of strong characters in
Davidson's drama—The Courtier in *A Romantic Farce*, Bruce, in
the play of that name, and the two heroes of *Smith*, for example.

These characters embody the essentials of the "Davidsonian hero." The hero typically affirms life; he despises the ennui and decadence of the late nineteenth century. Seeking a revaluation of decadent values, he replaces ennui with hard work and zealous living. He asserts his own character; indeed, self-assertiveness is almost a duty. He has a very high notion of his own worth, and he believes that he can control his environment. Being so strongly egoistic, he depends on his intuitions and emotions; and, as one might expect, he distrusts cold intellect. He prefers action to thought. Like a true Carlylean hero, he sees his duty and does it.

The hero's attitudes toward his fellow men are an extension of his feelings about himself. Because he is impatient with decadent society, he would remake it to bring it into line with his own vigorous assertiveness. And in the same way that he admires personal strength, he venerates national strength; therefore, the hero approves of empire building and offensive war. Might comes to mean right. In achieving his personal ends, the hero defies or ignores public opinion, moral codes, even laws, and he would have the nation do the same thing.

## II  *Irony and the Hero*

The Davidsonian hero's closest tie to the Davidsonian ironist is his individualism. Some of the portraits of the hero, especially early in the decade, are strongly colored by Davidson's ironic detachment. Furthermore, irony need not conflict with heroic vitalism, for the latter is not a doctrine or a dogma. As Eric Bentley says, "There is no creed of Heroic Vitalism. Heroic Vitalism is a faith, a dynamic *Weltanschauung*. In the details of application it adapts itself to the need of the moment." [4] It is a "point of view," a way of looking at life by which one may express his individuality. At midpoint in Davidson's career vitalism was not a dogma, though, as the decade of the 1890's progressed, Davidson's faith in heroic vitalism began to move toward the creed that it became in his later works.

An excellent example of Davidson's ironic treatment of the egoist hero occurs in the novel, *Perfervid: the Career of Ninian Jamieson*.[5] The hero, Ninian Jamieson, is as proudly egoistic as a hero could be: he has an idea that he can prove he is "legitimately, and by divine right, Ninian I., King of Great Britain, France, and Ireland" (44). He relates how he had long dreamed of taking over the throne by a military coup, or by simply announcing his identity and waiting for the country to crown him. But instead he read Carlyle's *Heroes and Hero-Worship*, and, he says, "I feel in myself the power to govern Britain as it has never been governed. I have the strength, if I can wrench from fate the opportunity, to weld together the English-speaking nations . . ." (48). He has gone so far as to have cast a medal with his likeness on the face "with the words 'NINIANUS PRIMUS, BRITANNIAE REX, F.D.' and on the reverse, the royal arms with 'GRATIA DEI, SED NON VOLUNTATE HOMINUM'" (49). Cosmo Mortimer, listening to Ninian's fantastic talk about the kingship, sums up the hero: "Ha, ha, ha! *Ninianus primus*—the prize ninny! Ha, ha, ha!" (54).

Ninian and Cosmo set forth on foot to take their chances and to try to regain the throne, but they have only gone a few miles when Ninian meets a girl and falls victim to a happy ending—and never carries out his plans. In any case, we see in Ninian, with his wild notions of his kingly nature, a man with an idea hardened into a dogma, one very much like Earl Lavender and also very much like the egoistic heroes of *Smith* and *Bruce*. But, unlike Smith and Bruce, Ninian is a first-class ninny. We need only recall at this point Davidson's professed "terror of doctrinaires and people with fixed ideas" to understand the duality in these satiric portraits—Davidsonian heroes treated with Davidsonian irony.

The egoistic hero, having great faith in his opinions and abilities, is always ready to reform society. Davidson treats the hero as a remaker of society ironically in a short story, "The Salvation of Nature," [6] which strongly suggests that heroic behavior is apt to be a bit ridiculous. The story begins by explaining what the hero has been doing by way of reformations:

> On the day that Sir Wenyeve Westaway's World Pleasance Bill became law, the happy baronet kissed his wife and said, "Lily, darling, it has taken twenty years, but we have saved Nature."
> "Never mind, dear," said Lady Westaway, who, though a true helpmeet, loved to quiz her husband, "the time has not been wholly wasted." (245)

The salvation of nature is to be brought about by buying Scotland; demolishing all foundries, railways, tramways, and other evidences of the industrial revolution (everything built after

1700); purchasing a number of the Polynesian islands; and spreading them over the razed cities, towns, and villages of Scotland. "When the land has thus been returned to the bosom of Nature, it will remain there unmolested for a year or two. At the end of this nursing-time, Scotland, having been in a manner born again, will be called by its new name, 'The World's Pleasance' . . ." (248); and it will become a great pleasure dome, a utopia, with even the weather controlled. Perhaps Davidson has Ruskin's St. George's Guild in mind.

The enterprise is such a huge success that it is repeated the whole world over. As a result, Nature is so upset that the entire human race dies except for two people, and they survive only through a lucky accident. Thus the remaker of society very nearly causes its total destruction. Aside from the implied criticism of social and economic planning, the story seems to say that Davidson is more than skeptical about the methods of reform and the uses of heroism.

### III  *The Hero as Individual*

But Davidson's forthright presentations of the heroic nature are much more numerous than his satires, especially after 1895. The underpaid clerk of the poem "Thirty Bob a Week" has the hero's philosophy of life. Though life may be hard going, he does not bemoan his fate (he may, however, complain a bit); rather, he hangs on to life, in spite of its precariousness, and fights to the end:

> It's a naked child against a hungry wolf;
>   It's playing bowls upon a splitting wreck;
> It's walking on a string across a gulf
>   With millstones fore-and-aft about your neck;
> But the thing is daily done by many and many a one;
>   And we fall, face forward, fighting, on the deck.[7]

This typically heroic nature, though he mixes his metaphors, embraces life; he despises weakness and lives dangerously and desperately, even if he is only a clerk. The overtones of Henley's "Invictus" seem apparent; and Browning, too, is in the background.

In both Davidson's roles—ironist and vitalist—he, like Henley or Browning, is scornful of the person who allows circumstances to force him into an atitude of unrelieved despair and weariness with life. Naturally, as a vitalist, Davidson would portray heroes who are able to control circumstances to their own best advantage; and this kind of hero figures prominently in several of Davidson's most famous poems. "A Ballad of Hell," for example, portrays a heroine who commits suicide and wakes up in hell only to discover that she has been deceived by her false lover who was to have committed suicide with her. But with the typical self-assertiveness of the vitalist,

> She marched across the floor of Hell;
>   And all the damned stood up to see.
>
> The devil stopped her at the brink:
>   She shook him off; she cried "Away!"
> "My dear, you have gone mad, I think."
>   "I was betrayed: I will not stay."
>
> Across the weltering deep she ran;
>   A stranger thing was never seen:
> The damned stood silent to a man;
>   They saw the great gulf set between.
>
> To her it seemed a meadow fair;
>   And flowers sprang up about her feet;
> She entered heaven; she climbed the stair;
>   And knelt down at the mercy-seat.
>
> Seraphs and saints with one great voice
>   Welcomed that soul that knew not fear;
> Amazed to find it could rejoice,
>   Hell raised a hoarse half-human cheer.[8]

The heroine, being a true vitalist, depends upon herself fully, and she is able by the force of her personality to mold circumstances to her desires. She is able to overcome all obstacles, moral, spiritual, even geographical (inasmuch as heaven and hell have a celestial geography). Or to put it another way, she reiterates the famous statement that "The mind is its own place, and in itself/ Can make a Heav'n of Hell, a Hell of Heav'n."

Like the heroine of "A Ballad of Hell," Davidsonian heroes generally depend largely upon intuition and emotion rather than upon rational logic, and they prefer action to thought. They are, in short, antirational. Like his heroes, Davidson often expresses his personal faith in intuition and emotion. For example, as early as 1889, he had praised spontaneity in writing, suggesting that literature is the more truthful the more spontaneous it is—a highly Romantic view of artistic creation and one which immediately recalls Wordsworth and Shelley. Davidson writes that "inaccuracy may be voluble, a lie may be glib; but neither can be spontaneous. Indeed, it may be said that spontaneity is the vesture of veracity, of that veracity which is clothed in mere accuracy of statement, as well as of the higher veracity of the imagination." [9] In another place, Davidson says defiantly: "I am the measure of the universe. I would cut my throat, if I, a thinking being, were ever compelled to doubt my own infallibility." [10] This statement is surely reminiscent of Blake, for whom reason is often the antagonist. For example, in "The Marriage of Heaven and Hell," the poet asks Isaiah, "Does a firm persuasion that a thing is so, make it so?" Isaiah replies, "All poets believe that it does. . . ." [11]

Sometimes Davidson's faith in emotion and intuition leads him to straightforward anti-intellectualism. In his novel, *Laura Ruthven's Widowhood*, 1892, Davidson says of the hero of the novel, "And so Meyrick is our hero. . . . We have faith in our heroine, and believe that, in the years to come, the lesson Meyrick Tunstall has learnt from her, that intellect is not everything . . . which so few, especially those who have any brains to brag of, ever learn, will make him a better and a wiser man—more tolerant and more human." [12] The anti-intellectualism which is implicit in the point of view of this passage is an important part of the nature of the hero; and it calls to mind the active heroes of Charles Kingsley's novels. Understandably, the hero who venerates emotion and intuitive behavior prefers action to thought, work to contemplation.

Besides explaining and clarifying the intellectual position of the heroic vitalist, Davidson also discusses and demonstrates the vitalist's relationship to other people and to society as a whole. Just as the hero deplores personal weakness and worships personal strength, so he deplores, as we have observed, national weakness and worships nationalistic power. At times, Davidson seems to be saying through various personae that "might" very nearly means "right."

In the long eclogue, "Lammas," published in 1895,[13] one of the speakers sets forth an idea which might best be described as he

describes it—a gospel of pride. He explains that his son will probably come to him in a few years, asking him why he is "weak, out-
classed, outcast" (34), unable to do anything great, without faith
in himself. The speaker, Ninian, is forced to be truthful, to tell his
son that it is due to the inherent weakness of the family: "Our
blood is stale; the tree from which we spring/ Fades at the top"
(36). Ninian blames his weakness on the world that makes "a
merit of defect, a cult of woe" (Christianity?), claiming it could
all have been remedied,

> If only nineteen hundred years ago
> A gospel of the pride of life had rung
> Our doleful era in; if the device
> In nature's choice of beauty and of strength
> Had then been showed to man, how had the world
> Approved the excellent expedient,
> With voluntary euthanasia
> Weeded humanity at once, and made
> A race of heroes in a golden age!
>
> (36–37)

This attack on Christianity sounds Nietzschean; it is strongly reminiscent of his *The Anti-Christ* or of his *The Genealogy of Morals*.
Yet we must go slowly in assigning an influence here; for, as I
have pointed out, Nietzsche's works were virtually unknown in
England until the first volume of English translations appeared in
April, 1896. Davidson's *A Second Series of Fleet Street Eclogues*,
in which "Lammas," from which I have quoted above, appears,
was actually published in December, 1895, though the title page
reads 1896.[14] Of course, we cannot discount the possibility of
Davidson's learning of Nietzsche's ideas through conversations
with translators or critics of his works, but neither can we conclude assuredly that Davidson knew a great deal more of Nietzsche
at the time of the writing of "Lammas" than what he had gleaned
secondhand from de Wyzewa's French article in 1891.

The ideas expressed in the passage quoted above have their
roots in evolutionary theory and in the application of evolutionary
theory to human relationships. When Ninian says that "nature's
choice" should have been demonstrated to man to show how nature weeded out weaklings, he undoubtedly means that "natural
selection" and "the survival of the fittest" should long ago have

been applied to men in order to rid mankind of its misfits—including Ninian himself (and also Davidson?). The implication is that Christianity is at fault for having propagated a culture which at least purported to favor the meek and the lowly and which includes as a part of its system of beliefs the notion that the meek shall inherit the earth.

However, Davidson, being typically ironic and noncommittal, puts this statement in an eclogue, where the mind can carry on a dialogue with itself and where he may set forth opposing ideas without seeming to give assent to either side. I discussed at some length how Davidson satirized Spencerian sociology in *Earl Lavender;* here he presents the other side of the case, taking the poet's prerogative to apply "any creed, philosophy, system of morality or immorality to life, and wring the utmost terror and beauty from its action." [15] Davidson has no doubt been reading his Darwin and his Spencer; however, there is no commitment, stated or implied, to the Darwinian viewpoint.

Furthermore, the speech is Ninian's, suggesting of course Davidson's own ridiculous hero with a fixed idea, Ninian Jamieson of *Perfervid.* Can we take it at all seriously? In any case, the worship of strength and the hatred of Christianity's "slave morality" are there, latent; the evolutionary belief in a super race is knocking about in Davidson's head, ready to be confirmed and crystallized, perhaps by Nietzsche's *Zarathustra.* And besides, in the same eclogue, "Lammas," Sandy, who in other eclogues represents the heroic vitalist point of view, advises Ninian to overcome his weaknesses by heroic self-assertion. Again the language and thought suggest Nietzsche, or Henley and Browning:

> Escape! I know the manner! Live at speed;
> And call your least caprice the law of God;
> Disdain the shows of things, and every love
> Whose stamen is not hate; self-centred stand;
> Accept no second thought; in every throb
> Your heart gives, every murmur of your mind,
> Listen devoutly to the trump of doom.
> You are your birthright; let it serve you well:
> Be your own star, for strength is from within,
> And one against the world will always win!
> (38)

Though spoken by one of the personae in an eclogue, the fact remains that Sandy's statement is almost a classic definition of heroic vitalism. Like Blake, Davidson says that the vital, active nature should ignore public opinion, stand self-centered, be one against the world.

In the same poem, we find Davidson experimenting again with the idea that suicide is the final triumph of individualism over circumstances, just as he had done in *Smith*. In a passage often quoted by Davidson's critics, Ninian is explaining that he has a manic-depressive nature, wavering between ecstatic happiness and gloomy despair. Thinking over his personality, Ninian says:

> I found that underneath indifference
> To every aim saving a livelihood
> My source of strength, though never to myself
> Confessed before, had been the lurking thought
> That passion, or a bullet, or the waves
> Could stop the unendurable ecstasy
> Of pain or pleasure, at whichever pole
> Of passion I determined to forsake
> The orb of life, on my acceptance thrust
> In ignorance and disregard of me,
> My temperament and fitness for the gift;
> But now that refuge of despair is shut,
> For other lives have twined themselves with mine.
>                          (32–33)

I have quoted at some length to put the passage in context, so that we do not take this as direct testimony from John Davidson that he had often thought of suicide. The speaker is Ninian (Ninny), and he has been commenting on his own mental aberrations. Nevertheless, Ninian expresses other ideas in the same poem which later reappear in other contexts with Davidson's full endorsement. The fact is that, though Davidson hides behind the persona of Ninian, he wishes to broach the concept of suicide as a way of demonstrating how man can control circumstances: by committing suicide, a man can at least die when he pleases. Suicide is a final act of heroic defiance.

## IV  *The Hero and Society*

Davidson's increasing tendency to worship power is illustrated in four poems published in 1898 and 1899, "The Aristocrat," "The

Outcast," "The Pioneer," and "The Hero," all of which relate the hero to society. By the late 1890's, Davidson had probably read *Zarathustra* with great care, and without a doubt his ideas about heroic behavior began to form themselves around the nucleus of Nietzsche's "will to power." As we have observed, John A. Lester, Jr., concludes that clearly Davidson had steeped himself thoroughly in the translations of Nietzsche's work as they appeared in the last years of the century.[16] What Davidson found in Nietzsche was not so much a new set of ideas as "a kindred spirit, facing kindred problems and driven by them to a similar view of the world." [17] Lester says that three of Davidson's ideas, which were indeed present before his reading of Nietzsche, were developed and intensified by the careful study of the German philosophers: Nietzsche's concept of the superman strengthened Davidson's concept of the value of heroism; Nietzsche's equating of sin and remorse with mental illness confirmed Davidson's fears of weakness; and Nietzsche no doubt crystallized Davidson's only partly articulated idea that Christianity was the cause of late nineteenth-century decadence.

At the present, our concern is with the first of these three ideas: the superman. The four poems I have mentioned portray a series of heroes who are more than heroic in the usual Davidsonian sense; they are barbaric, elemental, in tune with nature, especially "nature red in tooth and claw." The hero in "The Aristocrat" (1898) is a good example: he is a new-style aristocrat, really a plutocrat, a "money-lord," not a "warlord or churchlord"; and he is proud of it:

> Though Corner, Trust and Company
>     Are subtler than the old-time tools,
> The Sword, the Rack, the Gallowstree,
>     I traverse none of Nature's rules;
> I lay my yoke on feeble folk,
>     And march across the necks of fools.[18]

The aristocrat simply follows nature's rule of the survival of the fittest, as discovered by Darwin and Spencer. Might *does* mean right. The laws and rules of conventional society must bend before the heroic nature, who insists instead upon the absolute rightness of his intuitions. Though Davidson does not make clear how the hero is to gain his might, there is no doubt that Davidson is openly a hero worshiper, or, perhaps more accurately, a strength worshiper.

Thus, it is easy to see how, in deploring personal weakness and holding up personal self-assertiveness as a praiseworthy thing, Davidson is heading toward extreme nationalism and racial chauvinism. A series of poems and plays written between 1896 and 1900 show clearly that Davidson's heroic vitalism, as seen in the four short poems, was leading him toward a veneration of military might and toward the worst sort of jingoism. This development can be seen in Davidson's attitude toward England's empire building and involvement in European affairs at the end of the 1890's. The earliest treatment of the theme of England's empire building is the eclogue "St. George's Day," [19] in which social criticism is juxtaposed with rather extravagant praise of "good old Merrie England" as well as modern progressive England: thus the poem is an outstanding example of sustained ironic detachment.

Both sides of the question of the state of the English nation are held in suspension while the speakers in the eclogue toss ideas around. In the eclogue, Basil says he wants to sing "Of England and of Englishmen/ Who made our country what it is" (85); Herbert would sing "the praises of the English Spring" (87). Almost in chorus they celebrate their ancestry, real and legendary; they are sons of Robin Hood, Hereward the Wake, kings "Hal and Ned," and "Cromwell's Ironsides,/ Who knew no king but God above" (89). So far they have been expressing good-natured, openhearted, justifiable pride in England. Then Basil begins to praise "Greater England":

> St. George for Greater England, then
> The Boreal and the Austral men!
>
> (91)
>
> The Sphinx that watches by the Nile
> Has seen great empires pass away:
> The mightiest lasted but a while;
> Yet ours shall not decay.
>
> (96)

Thus it seems that we cannot determine beyond any doubt what Davidson thinks about empire at this time, for he is trying hard to be noncommittal. Yet empire building is given equal time, even though it is set alongside bitter criticism of England and her empire. Nevertheless, as I have noted in discussing the eclogue "Lammas" from the same volume, ideas which Davidson "tries out" in these poems have a way of cropping up later with his full endorsement.

Thus in flirting with ideas about empire and "might means right," and giving such ideas a lengthy airing, Davidson has begun to depart from the ironic detachment of *Perfervid* and *Earl Lavender*. His espousal of heroic vitalism and the breakdown of the ironic point of view occurs about the same time (1897–99) as the old desire to believe—the cat-call of the universe—begins to command more and more of his attention. Davidson's increasing commitment to heroic vitalism is evident in the three plays he wrote at the end of the decade of the 1890's: *Godfrida* (1898), *Self's the Man* (1899), and *The Knight of the Maypole* (1900).[20] Although these plays were written to make money (though they never did), they are peopled by vitalistic heroes and heroines.

In *Godfrida*, Davidson suggests that the ironic juxtaposition of good and evil, which he sees as the heart of the universe, is the theme of the play:

> . . . No felicity
> Can spring in men, except from barbèd roots
> Of discontent and envy deeply struck
> In some sore heart that hoped to have the flower.[21]

Possibly this ironic viewpoint is one theme, but given much more attention in the play are the extravagantly heroic protagonists, Siward, a medieval warrior, and his lady, Godfrida. Their behavior and their final coming together, despite the obstacles placed between them by Godfrida's jealous rival, supply the plot interest almost entirely. At the end of the play, they set off across the plains of France, but not until Siward has expressed his philosophy of self-assertiveness in a set speech, one which again calls to mind Henley or Browning:

> I cleft a passage through a hundred foes!
> Each nerve and sinew, every sounding pulse
> That marks the tramp of life along my veins
> Is charged to do my will triumphantly.[22]

The play, considered as a whole, shows clearly that the playwright has forgotten his professed theme of irony and has taken up the theme of heroic vitalism instead.

Davidson's next play, *Self's the Man*, written in 1899,[23] presents an equally self-assertive hero and adds a dash of jingoism. No doubt timed to capitalize on the wave of national unity and empire building that came during the Boer War (the play was published in 1901), Davidson's hero, Urban, a rival for the throne of medieval Lombardy, is an outspoken empire builder of the Clive-Hastings type. "My Lords," he tells the nobles, "it is with nations as with men:/ One must be first" (136); furthermore, Urban believes with Kipling that colonization is a moral obligation, the "white man's burden": "There lies/ A ruthless obligation on our souls/ To be despotic for the world's behoof" (136). Urban sees international relations in evolutionary terms as a struggle for survival. To the fittest will go the spoils:

> We must be first,
> Though everlasting war cement each course
> Of empire with our blood; or cease to be,
> Our very name and language in dispute.
> (136)

The overweening pride of which we see evidence in this speech is the cause of Urban's downfall. He is elected king but is dethroned when he tries to assume too much power. Exiled, he returns in the last act, twenty years after these events, to find that he is now a national hero, for hindsight has indicated he was right about expansionism. On the day of his return, a statue is being unveiled in his honor; and he finds Queen Sybil, his daughter, repeating the speech just quoted above to indicate what a wise king her father has been. Thus the whole play emphasizes and re-emphasizes the idea that nations must develop empires to survive. There is no ironic detachment apparent in this work, no effective opposition to the ideas of Urban. What opposition there is is proven wrong in the course of the play.

Thus Davidson's ideas about hero worship have come full circle; in the early period, in *Bruce* and *Smith*, Davidson venerated heroic, individualistic, egoistic behavior, although in *Smith* the praise of heroic behavior is somewhat moderated by Davidson's irony. At the beginning of the middle period, Davidson's assumption of a totally ironic point of view, his "terror of doctrinaires," brought him to satirize the egoistic heroes of *Perfervid* and *Earl Lavender* and the self-assured reformer of "The Salvation of Nature." But, in spite of the real or apparent ironic detachment, there was throughout the decade a serious presentation, which suggests endorsement, of the characteristics of the hero—self-assertiveness, individuality, the preference of action to thought, the reverence for intuition and emotion rather than intellect. Then in a series of statements and dramatizations, Davidson portrays the hero in society. Understandably, the hero is as ruggedly individualistic in public affairs as he is in his personal relations. From the poems and plays of the late 1890's, it seems evident that Davidson would apply the same sort of evolutionism, the notion of the survival of the fittest, to national and international affairs. If the fittest hero will survive, so will the fittest and most heroic nation.

## V   *The Hero as Outcast*

But, at the same time, there is good evidence that Davidson realized the dangers involved in his commitment to vitalism. As poet, he was intrinsically part of the great tradition of disinterestedness and critical detachment; and he remained enough of an ironist to the end of the decade of the 1890's not to wish to become a leader of a cause. Furthermore, he was aware of the spiritual risk of a total commitment to the egoistic hero's point of veiw; for extreme individualism may mean carrying a dependence on his own intuition so far as to sever all connections with the rest of the world, thereby losing touch with his audience, on the one hand, and with the great accumulation of human experience which had been the subject of his writing, on the other.

Davidson discusses this problem at some length in an essay published in 1898, "The Man Forbid." [24] In the essay the Itinerant is on the Downs again, his favorite place for confronting serious problems. There he meets "the Hermit, the Man Forbid, who neither hopes nor fears, nor hates nor loves." The Man Forbid has come to warn the Itinerant (Davidson?) to avoid his fate:

"What is your fate?"
"I shall tell you. I became so close a comrade of the day and the night and the time of year, so submissive a lover and student of men and

women, that I forgot all I had ever learnt from books. Then it seemed to me that I stood erect for the first time; and I looked with compassion on the multitude beside me, bent double under toppling libraries. I noted the heavier his load of libraries, and the more prone his attitude, the happier the porter seemed to be. I saw vast hordes of people engaged in tilling the soil, and in many other occupations, the majority of whom, whenever they could snatch an interval of leisure, spent it in grovelling under heavy burdens of printed matter, which, if they had none of their own, they would beg, borrow, or steal. 'Good people,' I cried earnestly, 'throw off your burdens and stand erect. Few are they who are helped by books.' " (297)

The Itinerant agrees with this last statement, and the Man Forbid continues his story. He found, as he explains to the Itinerant, that "there was no harbour for me among men. I left them, and gradually man and his fate became indifferent to me. . . . And all this— nay, I shall leave you with a smile—all this because I had cut my spiritual tail off. . . . It was a false analogy, that of the tail. Man grows out of the past; his tap-roots descend, drawing nourishment from every strata, and are warmed by the central fire. The scission of the smallest rootlet will hurt his growth" (297). The essay ends with an ironically understated summary of the Itinerant's (and Davidson's) problem: "The Man Forbid vanished as suddenly as he came; and the Itinerant pulled himself together. Had he thought of using the knife? He would consider the matter in his study. Meantime night was thronging into the sky" (297).

Considering that Davidson three years later chose to call one of his Testaments "The Testament of a Man Forbid" (1901), part of which is a rendering of this essay into blank verse, the essay becomes an important statement of his intellectual position. I have said that Davidson often praises the self-assertive, individualistic hero who is confident in his own intuitions and emotions. This hero has much of the ironist in him; he resists the restraints of public opinion, moral codes, or religions or other creeds; and he refuses to submit to any standard of behavior except that sanctioned by his own conscience. But, as ironist, Davidson also has the intellectual detachment to see that his position puts him in grave spiritual danger. One who rejects all traditions—moral, spiritual, literary, his history, in short—may well become a "man forbid," a man who loses contact with the rest of the world. Extreme individualism may well mean complete isolation, making it impos-

sible for him to be the "trembling lyre for every wind to sound"
that was his ideal of ironic detachment as stated in 1894. And this
very threat makes the essay so ominous: alone, on the Downs,
Davidson faces himself and predicts exactly what will happen to
him in the next decade. In short, he knows that his extreme individualism will overcome his detachment and make him a man
forbid.

## VI  *Irony and Heroic Vitalism: Some Conclusions*

Davidson's ideas during the decade of the 1890's seem to have
been following two rather divergent, almost dichotomous, patterns
of thought. On the one hand, Davidson's outlook in matters of belief was strongly ironic. He flatly refused to commit himself to a
cause, he said, because of his own great fear of doctrinaires: "To
me/ It now appears inept to take a side." [25] Yet the old problems
of belief were present. Though Davidson was, according to his
stated philosophy, suspending judgment, he could not ignore the
cat-call of the universe.

On the other hand, Davidson committed himself to a cluster of
ideas centering on heroes, hero worship, and heroic vitalism. In
fairness to Davidson, we cannot say that vitalism was his creed or
his doctrine—at least not during the first two-thirds of the decade.
During these years, he regarded heroes and heroic behavior with
a good deal of skepticism. However, as the decade progressed,
the ironic masks wore increasingly thin; and, by the end of the
decade, heroic vitalism had almost ceased being a faith and had
nearly hardened into a creed, one crystallizing around Nietzsche's
idea of the great man. Chronologically, we might note that con-
current with the recrudescence of the old problems of belief
(1897–1900), and thus implicitly the abandonment of the totally
ironic world view, came an increasing commitment to a creed of
heroism. Davidson even went so far as to suggest in *Self's the Man*
that might *does* mean right.

In a sense, the apparent contradiction between ironic detachment and faith in heroic vitalism can be explained by the ironic
frame of mind itself. Davidson claimed to be able to let the foulest
things lie at ease beside the loveliest, to accept the universe with
its contradictions. In this sort of juxtaposition lies the nature of
irony. Thus the ironist, theoretically at least, should be able to be

detached and committed to something at the same time. However, the obvious objection is that it simply cannot work; such negative capability cannot be sustained indefinitely.

The strong individualism that is at the heart of both sets of ideas is another obvious relationship. The ironist shares with the heroic vitalist a distrust of all standards of belief—perhaps we could omit "of belief"—choosing instead to trust his own conscience or his intuitions or emotions. We may venture to say that Davidson's own nature may account for the contradictions: at the heart of the matter is Davidson's "Scottishness," if we may use that word to describe a certain cultural heritage of protest and individualism.

R. M. Wenley, himself a Scot of Davidson's generation, makes several very acute observations in his introduction to Davidson's poems which underline what has already been said in Chapter 1 about the Scotch influence, the Scotch nature Davidson could not get rid of: "A nation [Scotland] saturated with the Old Testament Law and Prophets could hardly fail to breed incisive persons who, divining the transitive communal spirit, were bound to reveal unseen implications on a sudden, to prophesy and vituperate like Burns and Carlyle. Thus, Scottish religiosity, not as an ecclesiastical system, but as an attitude toward life, furnishes the clue to Davidson. Disavowing a creed, he could not disavow the cosmos." [26]

Wenley also comments with great insight about the peculiarly individualistic nature of the Scottish church: "The individual [Scotchman], while keeping within the bold periphery of Calvinism, learned to deem himself the vehicle of a 'higher law'—a conscience embodied in his own person as it were. He could therefore carry appeal to this tribunal from current 'abuses' in Church and State and doctrine: nay, to be plain, he did so on slight provocation." [27] In short, as Wenley says, "Davidson inherited [a] full share of the Protestant temper. He was a seceder by divine right." [28] The Protestant in him questions everything, and the Evangelical in him wants to believe in something. Perhaps it is logical for the ironist to be able to take refuge in the paradox of being a believer and an unbeliever at the same time; in a way, such a state contains an enormous contradiction; but, in another way, it is quite what Davidson might be expected to do. He might protest the creeds, but he could not ignore the universe.

Scotchman that he was, he rose to, and fought back at, the cosmos like a true heroic vitalist. In the next chapter, we shall see what happened when Davidson abandoned irony and proceeded "to prophesy and vituperate like Burns and Carlyle."

# CHAPTER 5

# *The Materialistic Message: 1901-1909*

> I wish to be most clearly under-
> stood:—Man is matter; mind and soul
> are material forces; there is no spir-
> itual world as distinct from the mate-
> rial world; all psychical phenomena
> are material phenomena, the result of
> the operation of material forces.
> —John Davidson,
> *The Theatrocrat*, 1905

EVEN during the period of his greatest detachment, Davidson wanted to say yes to something. The cat-call of the universe was demanding an answer; the ultimate questions were still re-curring. What is man? Where does he fit into the universe? What does life mean? Is there a God? And how do we find him? To these questions Davidson worked out materialistic answers. In the tradition of Burns, Carlyle, and his father, he became an evangelist with a message to an unheeding and unthinking world. In short, in the years from 1900 to 1909 Davidson completely abandoned his detached point of view and embraced a new creed as ardently as he had protested against any creed a few years before.

In 1903, Davidson described a "gaunt, dark man," a Davidson-ian ironist, for whom irony will no longer do:

"I," said the gaunt, dark man, "am he who determined to understand. Good and evil, right and wrong—these I thought, are the blinkers on the eyes of men by which Bigotry, Society, Use-and-Wont prevent their seeing too much in order to drive them more easily. I blamed nobody; I praised nobody; I neither loved nor hated; I would not punish; I would not reward; I would be intelligent and understand. And, indeed, everything and everybody became to me as clear as crystal. Yet I am full of terror and misery, and I know that I understand nothing at all." [1]

The last sentence points to an important reason for Davidson's search for a belief: paradox no longer affords refuge. Since Davidson could no longer sustain his detachment, he therefore set himself to find something to hold to. He still held to his heroic vitalism, but it did not explain "the relation of the Soul of Man to the Universe." [2] The search for this relationship is recorded in the Testaments and plays of 1901 to 1905—and again we find his development in his works.

I    *All Ideas in the Crucible:* The Testament of a Vivisector
*and* An Empire Builder

The final period and the search are begun in *The Testament of a Vivisector* (1901), a book so obscure and confusing that a well-meaning critic for the sporting newspaper, the *Star,* took it to be a satire on "vivisection, an infamy too gross for the common terms of scorn and contempt and abhorrence." [3] But the irony in *A Vivisector* is not satiric; it is, instead, the double-edged irony of an ironist whose detachment is so complete that he realizes he cannot sustain an ironic point of view. The intensity of the irony, as well as of the search for meaning in spite of the irony, shows through in the prefatory note: "This poem . . . and its successors, my 'Testaments,' are addressed to those who are willing to place all ideas in the crucible, and who are not afraid to fathom what is subconscious in themselves and others." He knows that "the new statement of Materialism which it contains is likely to offend both the religious and irreligious mind" (5).

Thus, Davidson invites, or commands, the reader to search with him for the answers to the cat-call of the universe. Appropriately, the series of books in which Davidson documents his search are called his Testaments, for they are clearly religious in tone and intention. They are the documents in a new covenant between man and the universe, the proclamation of the new creation that is in John Davidson's materialism. Davidson's Evangelical predispositions are evident in his new Testaments, and they remind us that he said in his will that "All men [should] study and discuss in private and in public my poems and my plays, especially my Testaments and Tragedies." [4] The picture of men's studying Davidson's Testaments and plays inevitably suggests "Bible study groups" or "midweek prayer meetings" dedicated to the understanding of the new gospel of matter. In these Testaments, the

Davidsonian ironist has given way to the Scottish Evangelical preacher, one burning with prophetic zeal.

In *The Testament of a Vivisector,* the speaker is a vivisector, though the dramatic mask scarcely hides the Davidsonian message. Man has a passion for knowledge, says the vivisector, because matter, of which he is made, drives him toward it. Matter has empowered man with thought only that he might have "self-knowledge" (10). In his own search for knowledge, the vivisector performs an experiment: he buys an old hack-horse, puts him to pasture, and waits for him to die. Finally, for two whole days the horse lies dying, but he is too full of the lust for life for death to win. "Where," the vivisector asks, "could the meaning of the riddle lie?" (19). How is it that this old gelded, dying horse still has a desire to live?

The vivisector concludes tentatively that the answer to life's riddles may lie in pain:

> Pain?
> It may be Matter in itself is pain,
> Sweetened in sexual love that so [*sic*] mankind,
> The medium of Matter's consciousness,
> May never cease to know—the stolid bent
> Of Matter, the infinite vanity
> Of the Universe, being evermore
> Self-knowledge.
>
> (26–27)

The experiment results in the above hypothesis. Pain may perhaps be in part the answer to the external question of what man's consciousness means; it may be matter's way of keeping man seeking for knowledge.[5] But *The Testament of a Vivisector* resolves no problems for Davidson, for the conclusion about pain is at best tentative and inconclusive. But the search is on, and the direction is suggested by the choice of a vivisector as persona and by the nature of the vivisector's experiment.

For a vivisector seeks to understand life by exploring the workings of living things. *Vivisection* suggests, as *Webster's Seventh New Collegiate Dictionary* puts it, causing distress to the subject; and vivisectors have long been criticized for their lack of humaneness. These very implications of vivisection accurately characterize Davidson's search for truth: the emphasis on seeking for truth in material things, the knowledge that his discoveries may cause pain and trouble, and his awareness of the criticism that is bound to rise from his material view of ultimate reality.

The stress in *The Vivisector* on the materiality of man's nature is a significant move in the direction of Davidson's final yes. Man is made of matter, he says; and this assertion becomes the ground of his entire materialistic philosophy. Also, the psychic process of thought is accounted for materially. Thought, says Davidson, is part of man's tendency toward self-conscious knowledge of its own nature. And, in a brief though important passage, Davidson says that perverted thought produced the ideas of God, heaven, and hell, which reduces these ideas from meaningful religious symbols to mere perversions of truth.

Yet Davidson is not going off into totally new directions for him; there are a number of connections with ideas from earlier works. For example, in the poem, "The Vengeance of the Duchess" (discussed in Chapter 3), Davidson has Casimir saying that "every atom in the earth/ Aches to be man unconsciously"—an idea closely paralleling the one in the *Vivisector* that matter's drive is toward self-knowledge. And, in the same poem, Casimir conjectures that all matter is pressing toward "that mood august wherein we know and suffer pain." [6] The similarity to the conclusion of *The Vivisector* is quite obvious. Though Davidson seems to be off on a different road—that of materialism—he has been on it before; but he has not decided as yet that matter counts for everything. The provisional conclusion of this first testament suggests that the quest for knowledge and certainty will continue.

Although the next testament to be considered, *The Testament of an Empire-Builder*,[7] is chiefly concerned with Davidson's ideas about empire, there are some signs of his continuing search for a belief. The poem is a monologue spoken by an empire builder, rather like the Urban of Davidson's play *Self's the Man* (see Chapter 4). The empire builder is dying. He muses that "Self-knowledge ends in self-contempt:/ Man can be too familiar with himself" (17)—a rather different idea from *The Vivisector*. The empire builder, clearly an imperialist, then relates a series of dream-visions in which he says that he saw the universe (18).

In the third and most important of the visions, he is wrapped in a cloud, carried away and left "standing on the verge of Heaven" (58), where he sees heaven and hell and their respective inhabitants (57–58). The traditional Christian ideas of these places are inverted: heaven is occupied by Davidsonian heroes; hell, by Christians. Although a full discussion of these ideas must await the first section of the next chaper, the empire builder's conclusions are relevant here: "Do I believe in Heaven and Hell?" he asks rhetorically; and he replies, "I do:/ We have them here; the world is nothing else" (78). As Townsend points out, "The poem makes it clear that these supposed afterworlds are no more than fictions for physical and psychological states." [8]

Thus Davidson seeks but arrives at no firm answers. A convocation of animals debates the problems of belief but makes no final statements. The empire builder sees that nature is cruel and red in tooth and claw, but Davidson had known that for a long time and had learned to accept it that way (see Chapter 3). The empire builder's heaven for heroes and hell for slaves is merely an extension of the philosophy of "might means right" which we know Davidson had held at least two or three years before writing *The Empire-Builder*. Therefore, all ideas remain in the crucible; the yes is yet to come.

## II   *The Everlasting Yea: "Man is Matter"*

In the fourth of the testaments, *The Testament of a Prime Minister*,[9] Davidson articulates fully his new creed of materialism. He has found a belief, and he takes it up as ardently as any revivalist ever embraced Evangelicalism. The "prime minister" of the title refers to the political office, but it also connotes that Davidson is the first (prime) spokesman (minister) of a new materialistic gospel (a new testament). The religious diction suggests something of the devotion that Davidson has hitherto shown in his pursuit of a belief, as well as the zeal with which he now sets out to preach the new gospel to every creature who will listen.

Though not published until late in 1904, Davidson wrote Grant Richards that *The Prime Minister* was "all ready" early in June, 1903, and that he needed only leisure to write it down.[10] Thus, the materialistic synthesis of the poem had been arrived at in mid-1903, not long after the publication of *The Empire-Builder* in mid-1902.

*The Prime Minister* is a monologue in which Davidson uses the mask of an English politician—in fact, Davidson later admits that the prime minister speaks for him [11]—though the choice of a prime minister does not seem germane to the poem aside from the fact that he is a strong character, a potential Davidson hero. The prime minister, like the empire builder, is dying. He had been a heroic character, "the heart and brain,/ Of Britain and her Empire" (6), above criticism, a true believer in himself, a Nietzschean overman. Yet he is assailed on his deathbed by doubts; like Davidson, he is still worried about God.

In telling about a speech made in Parliament, the prime minister clarifies the connection between heroic vitalism and the new-found materialism. He has argued that the Golden Age was about to return to England because men like him—proud, rebellious, free of restraints—had cast off the traditions which bound man to the Iron Age, and had finally achieved knowledge. This knowledge that he talks about is the heart of Davidson's message about the nature of man:

> For now at last we know, and all is now
> Permitted. Not an accident, nor made
> By any power demonic or divine,
> But Matter, Substance, Universe become
> Self-conscious. . . .
>
> ...............................................................
>
> Not God, nor Devil, but Material stuff
> That knows and thinks, imagines and despairs
> Endures and wills.
>
> (16–17)

Because man now knows he is material (since the prime minister has told him), he may be freed of the oppression of religious ideas of rewards and punishments in an afterlife, and seek his reward here; he may know that this age is Golden (25). He relates his theory of the "Golden Age" to this notion of a psychological heaven existing "here and now." The English, knowing this truth, will proceed to create their own heaven on earth, one made of good English gold. In this endeavor they will be assisted by Matter itself:

> *Get Gold, get Gold; and be the Golden Age!*
> So signals Matter from the ends of the earth
> Where'er her chosen people pitch their tents.
>
> ...............................................................
>
> One nation must be richer than the rest;
> Let it be ours!
>
> (26–27)

Matter, formerly expressing life unconsciously, but now self-consciously through the English nation, supports British imperialism.

The prime minister leaves the House of Parliament, overcome with emotion when he considers that humanity does not understand material truth. He walks along the Thames River, where he encounters a group of a dozen bums with whom he converses for a while. Like him, they are wondering what the universe is all about; they seem to have no answer. From the Thames embankment, he wanders into the forest. There, as evening falls, he hears vesper bells, and he enters a forest church, glad for the moment to seek again the shelter of the house of God. But, as soon as he begins to pray, he wonders whom he is praying to—the Hebrew God? Jesus Christ? a rich man's God? a God of the British Empire? Then the organ music brings about a vision of the cross of Christ which he interprets as "the death of God, the end of Sin" (78). This knowledge comes from his being "A Material soul/ At one with the Material Universe" (81). Although he sees a vision of God, there is no God, no heaven, no hell: [12] "I know that everywhere is Matter" (99). The ideas of heaven and hell are Matter's memories of the fires and catastrophes that took place in the ancient times when Matter existed only in the nebulae. Yet, after all of this talk, all the explanation of the visions, all the vehement assertion of the message, the poem ends on a note of doubt. On his deathbed, the prime minister still fears hell, still imagines the paradise of heaven, and still has "hideous dreams/ That wake me shrieking" (102). The dying prime minister finds cold comfort in the gospel according to John Davidson.

*The Testament of a Prime Minister* contains the entire Davidsonian gospel, though he has not at this time explored all of its implications. Man is matter, and all spiritual phenomena are explainable in material terms. One does not have to seek far for influences on Davidson's materialism. In the first place, there are the two years he spent in the laboratory in 1870 and 1871. There was an element of empiricism evident in Davidson's thought as early as *Diabolus Amans* in 1885, a tendency to believe in spiritual reality only when it may be measured by experience. As for intellectual influences, Davidson's reading in Huxley, Spencer, John Tyndall, and perhaps Ernst Haeckel and Ludwig Feuerbach, who are all associated with scientific materialism, or even Lucretius, may have helped develop his synthesis. Tyndall, for example, believed that "every structure and activity, mental as well as physical, on the earth, even our morality and art and science, were all somehow enfolded, as in a germ, in the primeval fire of the sun." [13] And, in spite of Huxley's protestations, many of his essays are materialistic: "The Phenomena of Nature," for example, claims that energy and matter make up reality; the entire universe, including man, is some combination of the two.[14]

Although Davidson is again not original, he nevertheless has the distinction of being the chief poetic spokesman for materialism; and he is surely one of few who made poetry out of atoms and electrons. From this time forth, materialism or some combination of materialism and vitalism are the subjects of nearly all his writings—poetry, drama, and prose. Like his poetic ancestor Blake, he had created for himself a new cosmography; but, unlike Blake, Davidson created no new myths. He was intent on destroying the old ones, and he believed it possible to talk about reality without using myth or symbol: as he put it, he wanted to "state the world." This "statement" as it is found in the Testaments is not particularly attractive.

If the Testaments have an appeal, it is chiefly to the intellect. If we read them (or keep reading) we do it because of their ideas, not because of their attractive presentation of the ideas. Undoubtedly the chief esthetic problem is that the testaments are obviously poems invented either to carry a thesis or to express the process of arriving at a thesis. They are propaganda, literature designed to teach; and the design is plainly apparent. Sir Philip Sidney says that "poesy must not be drawn by the ears, it must be gently led, or rather it must lead"; in the Testaments, Davidson has no doubt forgotten that to teach, literature must first delight.

Part of the problem is the confusion in point of view. Ostensibly the Testaments are dramatic monologues, but the dramatis personae—Vivisector, Empire Builder, and Prime Minister—have no existence independent of John Davidson. They all seem to be John Davidson in some mood or pose; and, if we called them all John Davidson, it would make no difference to the poems. Or, to put it another way, the poems are not dramatic monologues; they are dramatic diatribes.

Both the tortured language and the rigid verse form indicate the twisted monotony of these early Testaments. A glance at a page in the *Vivisector* turns up such words as *usufruct, alkahest,*

*solipeds* (23), as though expressing ultimate truths without symbols strains language to the limit. Inevitably, this kind of language
calls attention to itself and to the pressures on the Testaments to
propogate a message. But, if the language is somewhat freewheel-
ing, the verse form is rigidly blank verse with little of the subtle
variety which a Milton or a Wordsworth offers to make such verse
more than iambic-pentameter prose.

Yet we must more than grudgingly admire the strength and the
sheer force of Davidson's poetry. Though it does not measure up
as poetry, it does have a kind of visceral appeal. Somehow we feel
compelled to read on long after we have run out of forbearance, no
doubt because the message is after all so stoutly defended. Davidson's terrible honesty seizes us and holds us a good long while
and, if not quite all the way through, long enough for him to
communicate his message.

As we have seen, the core of Davidson's message is that man is
matter become self-conscious. By self-consciousness he means
(and I borrow Townsend's definition) "the conscious knowledge
by the universe of its origin, nature, and destiny as monistic and
material." [15] Matter's drive is, as Davidson says in *The Vivisector,*
inexorably toward this kind of self-knowledge, and only in man
has matter achieved self-knowledge. Thus, there is an evolution
toward higher consciousness in matter, according to Davidson, but
Darwinian evolution does not explain man fully. "I rate Darwin
higher than any other man who wrote in the last century," he
writes, "but in the meantime I do not believe that Natural Selection accounts for the origin of species. No beast was evolved out
of another beast. Matter tried again and again, and at last produced man." [16] Thus, matter has a will of its own, a will toward
self-knowledge; and it is almost another anthropomorphic god.

A full and carefully written prose explanation of materialism
appears as a long introduction to *The Theatrocrat,*[17] Davidson's
next book; and from it we gather the essentials of Davidson's materialistic creed. He repeats that man is matter: "Man consists of
the same Matter as the sun and the stars and the omnipresent
Ether; he is therefore the Universe become conscious; in him the
Universe thinks and imagines; and every man who trusts himself
trusts the Universe, and can say that which is" (24). A man is a
kind of microcosm; all the elements of which planets, moons, suns,
and earth are composed exist in man, as they do in all of Nature.

Man is different only in that he knows this fact, especially now that John Davidson has told him.

Because man is part of the universe, he may share its amorality and so free himself from conventions. "We know now that there is no moral order of the Universe, but that everything is constantly changing and becoming and returning to its first condition in a perpetual round of evolution and devolution; and this eternal tide of Matter, this restless ebb and flow, I call Immorality" (25). And again, "The Universe is immoral, and no sooner has a morality of any order established itself than the Universe begins to undo it" (26). Thus, Davidson's materialism confirms his questioning of established values.

Evangelical that he is, Davidson is not satisfied with cosmic amorality. He must lay the ghosts of God and of sin in order to have freedom from his troubled conscience. "I come now," he writes, "to the Material source of the idea of God" (68). As Davidson explains, the ether from which everything in the universe came fills all space and interpenetrates all matter, including man. The ether is something like air but is different in that it has in suspension all the elements which have been separated from it to make up the objects, organic or inorganic, that exist in the universe. Every people has tried in some fashion to express the presence of ether in them by projecting gods, or God, and a supernatural world. The material source of God, says Davidson, is twofold. One source is man's own ability to reproduce, to be in this sense immortal since his offspring are in effect flesh of his flesh. "The other source of the idea of God is in the Ether" (73). Every atom of man is made out of the ether, in fact is "saturated with it; therefore man is "Ether become conscious" (73). And so man's memory of his ethereal origin prompted him to think that "Out of God he came . . . and back to God he should return" (74); but the truth is that he shall return to ether, not God. According to Davidson, man "is the Ether, condensed, evolved; and . . . he will devolve again into that invisible, imponderable form of Matter' '(74). Or stated another way: in the beginning was the Ether, and the Ether was God.

Sin also may be explained in material terms. Conviction of sin is "the effect of the exhaustion of the Material forces of the Matter of man" (65). Man thinks of sin only after the act, Davidson argues. "Sin, then, is . . . the transference of the title Sin from the impotence of the spent Matter to the energy that was expended" (66). Sin and a bad conscience are thus explained physiologically: sin in a sense is the lack of the ability to do something sinful. The connection here with Davidson's heroic vitalism will be discussed more fully in the next chapter. I might note, however, that, from the frequent references to doubts and uncertainties, Davidson probably had a difficult time persuading himself of the materiality of sin. The old Calvinism hung on.

Heaven and hell could more easily be explained to fit the material creed. Out of the all-pervading ether first came atoms, formed by lightning, the poles of which created the many oppositions in the universe, such as the sexes and the positive and negative charges of electricity. The atoms then united into matter, and the matter formed itself into one great nebula. "The next important event," Davidson writes, "is the condensation and contraction of the nebula with the segregation of planets, when all the chemical affinities, the energies of electricity and heat, radiative action, centrifugal and centripetal forces and the force of gravitation kept up for millions of years a war of the elements no atom of Matter can ever forget" (41). From this eon-long conflict man's ideas of eternity are derived: "The blood, the brain, the bones, the flesh, and the marrow, retaining an indelible impression of their placid existence in the unbegun Ether, of the diaphanous light of the nebula, and of the terrific time of infernal tumult when the solar system was evolved, suggested to man, when his highly developed consciousness begat a still unenlightened idea of the Universe, that splendour on high, his glowing Heaven of light, and that horror below, his fiery Hell of torment" (41). The idea of heaven is, therefore, an atomic memory of the placid pre-nebula days; that of hell, of the molecular tumult that formed the universe.

Davidson seems to say that the traditionally symbolic religious language does not symbolize anything. He does not want to reinterpret or to explain the symbols, but to get rid of them. His material view of the universe negates the need for symbols, since he knows what the universe *is*, not what it is *like*.

If Matter explains away heaven, hell, God, and sin, it may also clarify other nonobjective realities. For example, creativity, which Davidson cited as evidence of the immaterial nature of reality in *Diabolus Amans* (see Chapter 2), is explained in 1905 as an expression of matter's consciousness. "Thus poetry, like an artesian

well, broaches the heart of Matter directly, and is its most inti-
mate expression. . . . Without any intermediary . . . and condi-
tioned only by language, the poet can utter that which is: the
heart and the brain, the flesh, the bones and the marrow—Matter
become sub-conscious, conscious, and self-conscious. . . ." [18] This
explanation is in fact a materialistic version of what Meyer Abrams
has labelled the "expressive theory" of poetry, the typical Romantic theory that the poet is the most sensitive of men and that the
function of art is to express the poet's mind.

However, Davidson goes so far as to state that matter has its
say, willy-nilly, in speaking through the poet: "Poetry is Matter
become vocal, a blind force without judgment. Much there is a
poet can control; . . . but the purport of his poetry is not within
his own control." [19] We might say, therefore, that poetry is the
spontaneous overflow of matter's self-consciousness. Davidson argues that Milton, for example, set out to justify the ways of God
to Man, but he ended by expressing the voice of matter when he
made a heroic Satan. "Matter says its will in poetry; above all, in
English blank verse, and often, as in the case of Milton, entirely
against the conscious intention of the poet." [20]

According to Davidson, matter developed blank verse especially
for the English: "English blank verse came into being when a new
mode of expression was needed. . . . This English race, having
thrown off the fetters of a worn-out creed, having obtained the
kingdom of the sea and begun to lay hands, as by right, on the
new world, burst out into blank verse without premeditation, and
earth thrilled to its centre with delight that Matter had found a
voice at last." [21] He concludes that "Matter nowhere in the Universe has evolved anything transcending mundane man, or a
nobler utterance than this very blank verse." [22]

In summary, matter explains God and man; the expending of
matter explains sin, and matter's memory of creation explains
heaven and hell. Man's ideas of immortality derive from the fact
that he ultimately came from the ether and to ether he shall return. Even man's highest expression, poetry, results from matter's
self-consciousness in man.

When we consider all the quasi-scientific jargon (and a great
deal more could be quoted), we are tempted to label Davidson
merely an opportunist who tried to make poetry out of the imagery
of science and the scientific hypotheses. On the other hand, it is

apparent that much exists in his statements that is not "scientific," not verified by experiment and probably not verifiable, as, for example, the highly subjective theory of poetry. Davidson, who readily admits this fact, disclaims an attempt to build an orderly system: "I have no system; I have no dogma; it is a new poetry I bring." [23] He suggests that he is transcending science: "In the course of many ages the mind of man may be able to grasp the world scientifically: in the meantime we can know it only poetically; science is still a valley of dead bones till imagination breathes upon them." [24] What Davidson proposes is a scientific hypothesis arrived at through a poetic apprehension of reality; what happens is that his poetic view of the universe becomes a creed.

### III  *The Death of God and the Attack on Christian Ethics*

In *The Testament of a Prime Minister,* the Prime Minister witnesses in a vision the death of God. Significantly, the vision comes in a church to which the Prime Minister had gone to pray, "as some lost soul from deep perdition snatched"; [25] and the incident surely suggests that Davidson would have liked to turn to the church for the security of its beliefs. As through the aisles of the church pass "the pageant and the obsequies of Sin" (79), the Prime Minister conceives that he is the first to understand the full implication of the crucifixion:

> The esoteric meaning of the Cross—
> That God gave up the ghost on Calvary,
> And bore away the Sin of all the world?
> How could mankind perceive until today
> That God and Sin existed not at all;
> That with the death of Christ there also died
> The two insane ideas, God and Sin?"
>
> (80)

We should note carefully that the *ideas* of God and sin died; the materialist Davidson must of course never admit that there is (or was) a God. The idea of God died on Calvary, and Davidson would proclaim this new gospel of the "Death of God" to the world.

Davidson's portrayal of the death of the idea of God is not surprising. As early as 1885 in *Diabolus Amans* he had set forth a subjective God who had no absolute existence outside man's concept of Him. Because man believed in God, there was God; and now that he no longer believes, it is easy for him to say there is no God. During the 1890's Davidson was reticent about his ideas of spiritual reality. His ironic detachment allowed him to use traditional Judeo-Christian mythology without committing himself on the questions of belief. In view of his declaration of materialism, which finds its fullest statement in *The Prime Minister,* the denial of the reality of anything numinous follows quite logically. His material explanation of God calls for some sort of explicit rejection of the subjective God which he had earlier admitted. The scene from *The Prime Minister* thus symbolically frees Davidson from his own emotional, intuitive beliefs.

The death of sin which accompanies the death of God is also necessitated by the material explanation of the universe. In *Diabolus Amans,* Davidson had said clearly that "Sin is sin/ And he who sinneth hath begun to die." [26] And in order to atone for his sins he turned to good works. In the 1890's, however, Davidson adopted an ironic view of the universe in which good and evil were reversed and in which moral relativism replaced the absolute of sin. In a few cases, such as in the poems of social criticism, there was an implicit acceptance of Christian ethics ("St. George's Day"); in others, such as the imperialistic verse and drama, the Christian ethic gave way to a gospel of strength. Now Davidson's materialistic synthesis requires not only that he portray the death of sin but also that he show how Christian morality prevents man from being in harmony with a material universe. Thus, the task that he sets for himself is nothing less than persuading the world that sin did die on the cross, that the twenty centuries of Christianity have been misdirected toward a dead folklore, and that it is high time for man to leave behind him what he considers the outmoded, decadent Christian ethic and to "live no longer in a myth but in the Universe itself." [27] Thus, Davidson's attack is leveled chiefly at Christian ethics, not theology. He assumes that his materialism, as well as modern scientific discoveries, will show people that "the study of God . . . [is] a branch of mythology." [28] Yet the ethics of Jesus Christ would not so easily give way before the onslaughts of scientific materialism: even Huxley and Darwin wanted to retain Christian morality.

But Davidson did not. "Is there any thinking person who does not wish to see the world made over again?" he asks in 1905. "Men tinker and patch with policies and economics; but it is Christendom that is the matter with the world. The world is sick of Christendom. We must come out of Christendom into the Universe." [29] At this time his attack on Christianity is no better articulated than in this statement; therefore, discussion of his full critique of Christendom must await the survey of the Mammon plays in the next chapter. In them, he shows what he believes is specifically wrong with Christianity and what a materialist does about it.

Meanwhile, Davidson knew he had a big job on his hands, one that he explained to William Archer in 1904:

My purpose in these Testaments is to aid in the overthrow of the rotten financial investment called Christendom: I perceive that this can be done only by purging the world of everything that is meant by spirit, soul, "other" world, though all the literature and art and religion of the past should go with it. I would start the world over again from the only mystery, Matter.

All this clarifies in the play I am writing: it is terrible also: it half kills me to write it. Fiend! I will make you know I can write a play. It will be saturated with this Matter of mine, and therefore unlicensable, and I will take license further to get my matter stated. . . .[30]

The play Davidson refers to is *The Theatrocrat*,[31] written in 1904.

### IV *The Materialist as Outcast:* The Man Forbid *and* The Theatrocrat

"I have repeatedly attempted to speak this that I am writing," Davidson wrote in the Introduction to *The Theatrocrat*, "and have always failed, coming out of it in a dumb rage." [32] Nevertheless, he had to speak. *The Theatrocrat*, 1904, is a play in which Davidson dramatizes two things: his message and the difficulties that he knows will ensue in persuading men to accept it. *The Theatrocrat* is almost entirely in blank verse, a very few . hexameter lines excepted. This verse form is followed so faithfully that even telephone conversations are in blank verse. This rigidity of form suggests the inflexibility of Davidson's mind at this time: his materialistic unorthodoxies have hardened into an absolutely uncompromising new orthodoxy. However, before we examine *The Theatrocrat* we should backtrack briefly and note that Davidson was preoccupied with the difficulties involved in expressing his ideas well before his materialism was fully evolved.

The second of Davidson's Testaments is *The Testament of a Man Forbid*,[33] published in 1901 shortly after *The Vivisector*. It is a poetic rendition of the prose essay discussed at the end of Chapter 4, with, however, one very important difference: Davidson clearly identifies himself with the "Man Forbid." In the essay, he sustained a measure of objectivity in his discussion of the problems of ideological isolation by casting himself as the Itinerant who interviews the isolated character, the Man Forbid. Though *The Testament of a Man Forbid* is a monologue, supposedly spoken not by John Davidson but by a persona, there is no doubt in the reader's mind that the Man Forbid is a person very like John Davidson. This Testament gives some indication of how aware Davidson was of the problems which he faced in working what is nothing less than a reformation of the basic value system of Western civilization.[34]

"I . . . began to think what it was I wanted in the world," he writes in an essay in 1905. " 'Have you,' I said to myself—'have you lessened your claim since you were a boy?' 'No'—I deliberated over the answer: 'no; it is still to me a deep disgrace that I have not the command of an invincible army and the spending of the revenue of the United Kingdom.' " [35] Since Davidson did not have the army and the revenue, he sharpened his pen for the conflict and wrote a play. He called his play *The Theatrocrat*,[36] and in it he set forth his message in a prose introduction and in the play itself.

The problem of telling a hostile audience about the gospel of materialism looms large in the play: in fact, *The Theatrocrat* predicts its own failure; [37] for, in the play within the play, Davidson's messenger of materialism is killed by his own angry audience.

In *The Theatrocrat*, Sir Tristram Sumner, once a successful London actor and producer, determines against all advice to produce Shakespeare's *Troilus and Cressida*. His wife, once beautiful and talented but now degraded and neurotic, is sure that Warwick Groom, once her lover, must do Troilus if the play is to succeed. But when Groom appears intoxicated on opening night, the play fails, and Sir Tristram goes bankrupt. At this point, the Bishop has a message to deliver and prefers the theater to the pulpit—and thus ends the first three acts. What happens in the last two acts is important in this study; for as Davidson says in his Introduction, "St. James's message . . . is also mine: my statement of the world, and of the Universe as the world can know it" (24). St. James's message is clearly Davidson's creed of materialism and of anti-Christianity, and he states it to Sir Tristram with what becomes tiresome repetitiveness (it takes him ten pages) "Still I say it, and again/ And yet again it must be said" (144).

Davidson's choice of the Anglican Bishop of St. James's as his persona and mouthpiece again underlines his religious dedication to the message of matter. St. James's (Davidson uses the form *St. James's* in the nominative all through the book), like Davidson, no longer believes in God; and like Davidson, he is a Man Forbid, having spent some time in exile (140 and 147). There he has written a play which contains a message, a new creed.

Davidson's use of the stage as a sounding board for his ideas undoubtedly shows the influence of Henrik Ibsen and George Bernard Shaw. The harsh Realism of some of the subplots of *The Theatrocrat*, for example, especially brings to mind Ibsen; but we must also note the Romantic touch, surely unlike Ibsen, of Lady Sumner's supposed clairvoyance. Though Davidson's attempt to solve problems through the drama places him in the tradition of Ibsen and Shaw, the verse form and the Romantic extravagances relate the play more to late nineteenth-century imitations of Shakespeare and melodrama.

Dramatic tradition was one of the things Davidson had in mind when he named the play *The Theatrocrat*, a word which he coined and one which has several definitions in the context of the play. First, Sir Tristram Sumner is clearly supposed to be the "Theatrocrat" (101 and 111): he is a leading London player, producer, and theater owner. The state has knighted him, and the church has praised him (112). Thus "theatrocrat" is clearly a blend of *theatre* and *aristocrat*, and a theatrocrat is a ruler of the theater. Second, Sir Tristram has also been ruled *by* the theater: he has subordinated his convictions as well as the potentialities of the stage to personal fame and applause. These signs of his degeneracy are emphasized by his wishing to produce *Troilus and Cressida*, which Davidson regards as a decadent play.

JOHN DAVIDSON

Third, there is no doubt a parallel between *theatrocrat* and *theocrat*. If a theocrat is one who governs, or supports the government of a state by a powerful church which forces its creed upon everyone, then a theatrocrat is one who would use the power of the theater to force his creed upon his audience. In the play, this sense of *theatrocrat* is illustrated by Davidson's mouthpiece, the Bishop of St. James's. Finally, and perhaps most important, the word *theatrocrat* is related to the rare word *theatrocracy*, which according to the *Oxford English Dictionary* means "absolute power exercised by the ancient Athenian democracy, as exhibited at their assemblies in the theatre; ochlocracy." A theatrocrat, then (the *Oxford English Dictionary* does not have it in that form), would be a supporter of government by the mob or the lowest of the people, as exhibited at an assembly in the theater, or in other words, a member of the theater audience who exercises absolute domination over the playwright. In one important sense, Davidson means by *theatrocrat* the audience, both the audience of the play within the play, St. James's audience (which murders him), and the readers of *The Theatrocrat*, Davidson's audience (which dominates and threatens to ruin him).[38] The theatrocrats have already made him a Man Forbid, and the play predicts an even worse outcome for the founder of the new theology of matter.

Act IV portrays the opening night of the Bishop's materialistic play. The play within the play takes place offstage during this act and is reported by various people. We learn that St. James's speaks the prologue and that it goes over very well. But the initial success is too much for the Bishop; accustomed to the cathedral, not the theater, he is carried away by his responsive audience, and is said to be "discoursing Matter like a thunderstorm" (173). "All is Matter, all," the Bishop cries to the audience; and then some one asks him, "What price God?" (174). When the blasphemous message of matter breaks forth from St. James's, the members of the audience—parson, moneylender, broker, banker, peer, duchess, milliner, wife, prostitute—rise as one person and smash the theater in the name of God (174–75).

Act V, which opens on the wrecked stage as the last members of the audience leave the theater, finds the Bishop of St. James's lying unconscious; and, as the play ends, he dies of wounds sustained in fighting the good fight; but he is envisioning, nonetheless, matter's great kingdom,

> A greater breed of men, a nobler world
> An omnipresent power in the Universe,
> The Universe itself become aware.
>                                    (195–96)

The implications of St. James's death are many. In the introduction Davidson had written, "My statement of the world and of the Universe as the world can know it has offended and will offend; but I have no purpose of offence; nor am I concerned to please: my purpose is to say that which is, to speak for the Universe" (24). Although he looks forward to the victory of materialism, he realizes that the revaluation he desires may engender a millennium of strife: "This war will last a thousand years," says the bishop as he lies dying (193). In fact, he says, a whole new value system may have to be forced upon humanity before it can accept his message. "We must have a new world in order that the utmost may once more achieve itself in literature. If it were only that there might be a new drama it would be necessary to have a new cosmogony."[39]

Thus the message and its means of expression are interdependent. Both are new, and neither will easily replace its predecessor. Nevertheless, the change is inevitable, Davidson believes optimistically. According to a conversation between Sir Tristram Sumner and the Bishop of St. James's, which follows St. James's first profession of materialistic faith, England is about to enter another Golden Age, when, as in the Renaissance, the poet's imagination will be stirred by new discoveries and by an expanding empire; and there will be room for a new drama. In response to William Archer's review of *The Theatrocrat* in the *Daily Chronicle*, Davidson explains further: "My play is the first step towards this new drama. Mr. Archer, applying to my play a theory of the drama based upon a knowledge of the dramatic literature of the world, inevitably finds it inconceivable and undramatic. My play must be judged by its own theory; there is nothing else to judge it by; it begins the world over again." [40]

Though what Davidson says is optimistic in tone, there is nothing optimistic about the play, especially the last two acts. For example, in St. James's loss of control over himself and in his being carried away by the materialistic message, we find a suggestion of how the new orthodoxy obsesses John Davidson. If St.

[ 103 ]

James's had stuck to his prepared prologue, which the audience liked, he would have been safe; and his audience would have stayed to see the play. But with a kind of terrible self-knowledge, Davidson portrays a hero who is swept away by his message, and the play within the play fails not even grandly but miserably before it ever gets a hearing. The message generates its own sort of spontaneous overflow, and Davidson seems to say that he knows how apt he is to forget the art and concentrate only on the message, even though his own success and his family's well-being might be at stake. The play within the play foreshadows Davidson's Mammon plays which followed in 1907 and 1908. In them, he attempted what St. James's attempts: the overthrow of Christianity and the establishment of the religion of matter.

More than this, St. James's failure foretells Davidson's failure, and his death at the hands of a hostile audience is a kind of prophecy of the suicide of John Davidson. The theatrocracy, the people, triumphs over the theatrocrat, St. James's-Davidson, who tries to use the theater as a rostrum for a message of materialism.

In summary, *The Theatrocrat* draws together and restates the creeds evolved in the Testaments. It is also a dramatization of Davidson's method of preaching the gospel of materialism to every creature and of his intentions to use his art to teach. But, more than that, the play is also an augury of Davidson's future: he will write plays; he will present his message in these plays; what audience remains will rise up almost to the man to silence him.

### V  *Looking Forward: Heroic Defiance*

In 1905, Davidson had a few years of struggle left in him; he was not ready yet to submit to the hostile theatrocrats. He expressed his proud, almost haughty defiance of fate in his best poem, "A Runnable Stag," first published in 1905, about the same time he was writing the prose introduction to *The Theatrocrat*.[41] In "A Runnable Stag," a monologue spoken by a hunter, the persona successfully masks the poet; for the stag, not the hunter, most objectifies the character of John Davidson. The simple idea of the poem is stated with dignity and grace:

> When the pods went pop on the broom, green broom,
>   And apples began to be golden-skilled,
> We harboured a stag in the Priory coomb,

> And we feathered his trail up-wind, up-wind,
> We feathered his tail up-wind—
> > A stag of warrant, a stag, a stag,
> > A runnable stag, a kingly crop,
> > Brow, bay and tray and three on top,
> > A stag, a runnable stage.
>
> (14)

But the poem need not be read as a commentary on Davidson's life or ideas. The poem expresses clearly and skillfully the unconstrained and unconstrainable freedom of a noble animal. The poet suits the meter and rhythm of the poem to the rhythm and excitement of the hunt without allowing the poem to become merely a clever tour de force, a display of virtuosity. The alliteration also suggests the rhythm as well as the inevitable repetitiveness of a hunt that goes for thirty miles across the country. And, when the poem ends with the stag sinking to his jeweled bed under the sea, it closes in a noble, regular rhythm, and the regular thundering of the heavily accented syllables is muted and changed into a quiet dignified close.

Looking once more at the poem in the context of Davidson's development, we see him predicting (almost) the opposition he will meet and, more tragically, even predicting the way he would commit suicide. Yet, in spite of what lies ahead, Davidson defies the fate that he seems to know clearly is his. There is something in us, in me at least, which grudgingly admires such courage. In the next chapter we shall see, however, that the stag was not run down in 1905, for Davidson had not said all that he wanted to say.

# CHAPTER 6

## *Materialism and Heroism: 1901-1909*

> I'll carve the world
> In my own image, I, the first of men
> To comprehend the greatness of mankind;
> I'll melt the earth and cast it in my mould,
> The form and beauty of the universe.
> ............................................................................................
> Yet must our battle-cry be as I said,
> "Get thee behind me, God; I follow Mammon."
> —Mammon, in John Davidson's *Mammon and his Message*

IN his poems and plays written in the late 1890's, Davidson spoke more and more about a philosophy of "might means right." His hero worship became worship of strength—often of the strength of a nation to wage war. During the years from 1901 to 1908, he became increasingly a worshiper of power; and his belief in heroism reached a peak in the so-called Mammon plays of 1907 and 1908. And, most importantly, during this period Davidson tried to work out a synthesis between his two philosophies: heroic vitalism and materialism. In fact, though they contradict each other in some ways, Davidson overlooked these contradictions and made each concept complement the other. He fused his hero worship with materialism to produce a new hero—the hero as materialist.

## I  *A New Ballad of Heaven: The Testament of an Empire-Builder*

In the third of the dream visions in *The Testament of an Empire-Builder* (1902),[1] the empire builder stands on the verge of Heaven (58), where he sees the inhabitants of an Eden-like paradise: they are heroic vitalists, those who fought hard, defied fate, trusted their emotions and intuitions. They are a veritable catalogue of Davidsonian heroes—iconoclasts, nonconformists, imperialists, warriors, kings, popes, dishonest brokers, robbers, suicides. Besides these, there are a great many heroic women, chiefly those who mastered men, but also those who accepted as good and right their natural sexual abilities, not only "mothers beautiful as dawn," but king's mistresses and "harlots of the street in joyful herds" (63). Those he saw in heaven were, in short, "all who challenged fate and staked their lives" (65).

The empire builder then seeks for hell, the place where heretics, suicides, and adulterous lovers are supposedly punished. There is no hell, he thinks; but the beautiful music he hears in heaven suggests that its opposite exists somewhere: such pleasure must have its complement of pain. He beholds, seated in the midst of heaven, a celestial organist, playing on a "jewelled keyboard on a jasper plinth" (71). Looking beyond the organist, he sees at the outermost edges of heaven what appears at first to be a nebula, then a tapestry embossed with human eyes, then a cliff encompassing heaven. But finally he realizes that this is a hellish amphitheater, constructed of the inhabitants of hell. In Dantesque imagery, the empire builder describes how these people are, as it were, frozen into position,

> Except that groups and terraces of folk
> Distended myriad mouths for every key
> The gracious player struck.
> (73)

Heaven is entertained by music made out of the screams of the damned, and the damned are the unheroic, those who do not subscribe to Davidson's philosophy—altruists, agnostics, dreamers, idiots, cripples, dwarfs, cowards, Christians, and "the greater part/ Of all the swarthy all the tawny tribes" (77). As the vision ends, the empire builder happily proclaims his joy at seeing Lazarus in hell and Dives in heaven, an arrangement proper to the gospel according to John Davidson.

The empire builder has been on the side of the angels all the time, for blessed are those who join "the warfare of the times/ In corner, trust, and syndicate." His mastery of fate and circumstances is easy because he is English, "one of the elect," he says (79). His parting word of advice to the English is a monument to excessive nationalism:

The English Hell
For ever crowds upon the English Heaven.
Secure your birthright; set the world at naught;
Confront your fate; regard the naked deed;
Enlarge your Hell; preserve it in repair;
Only a splendid Hell keeps Heaven fair.

(81)

In *The Testament of an Empire-Builder,* three ideas important to the writings of the later years are clear. First, Davidson more strongly praises the British Empire than he had at any time before. Second, he says that the English are an elect nation, foreordained to be a great world power. Third, he inverts not only Christian mythology but also Christian ethics. Evil and good are not synonymous, but rather evil is good and good is evil. We have no longer a marriage of heaven and hell but a complete reversal. Although *The Empire-Builder* deals with these ideas, they are developed in other ways in other of Davidson's works of the period—poetry, prose, and drama—to which we now turn.

## II  *Might Means Right: The Poetry of Empire*

On August 9, 1902, when Edward VII was officially crowned King of Great Britain and Ireland and of the British Dominions Beyond the Seas, and Emperor of India, John Davidson published an "Ode on the Coronation of Edward VII., of Britain and of Greater Britain, King." [2] The ode is a paean to the predestined British Empire, or so Davidson sees it. He outlines a short history of England up to the Boer War in which the whole British Empire rose up in a time of need, "Imperial Britain, mighty and aware" (10). Britain is great because of her people, who are in fact, though they may not know it, Davidsonian heroes: "Doers, endurers, fighters, poets, kings,/ The genius of the Universe..." (11). Perhaps we may charge some of the ode's excesses to the occasion of the coronation, but Davidson chose to reprint the poem a year later without changing its tone. Obviously, he strongly supports British imperialism and cites in its favor the inherent greatness of the English, their preordained destiny as a power in world affairs.

One of the three epigraphs to the poem as it appears in 1902 is a quotation from *The Origin and Destiny of Imperial Britain* by John Adam Cramb,[3] a book accurately described as "a defense of

British imperialism along evolutionary lines." [4] No doubt this book by Cramb, a professor of modern history at Queen's College, London, helped Davidson formulate his notion of the imperialistic destiny of Britain. Writing to Edmund Gosse on December 24, 1900, Davidson praises the book highly as "the ablest, freshest, most imaginative and therefore most intelligent statement of British Imperialism, and a revelation of the development and future of that idea only possible to a man of genius." [5] Clearly, Davidson agrees with Cramb's theses regarding the superiority of England and its genius for empire building.

Several poems in 1906 in Davidson's *Holiday and Other Poems* are hymns to the British Empire: "Merry England," "The Twenty-Fourth of May," "Our Day," and "New Year's Eve." The least unattractive of the four poems is "The Twenty-Fourth of May," [6] an eclogue in which Davidson reverts not only to the poetic form which he had used so successfully during the 1890's but also to something of the ironic point of view. In the poems, Basil and Lionel praise the empire, but Brian questions it. Basil says that Brian need not worry about the civil wars caused by empire; that sort of thing happens only in landlocked empires, where empire means restriction. Since Basil has the last word, the empire receives more praise than blame. But the poem is at least not so blatantly jingoistic as some other things Davidson was writing at about the same time, such as "New Year's Eve," another eclogue in the same volume of poems, in which something of the violence of war that inevitably accompanies empire building comes through.

In fact, Davidson seems to approve of war more and more readily as he grows older. In 1903, he writes aphoristically and rather obscurely, "To understand all is to fight and slay. War, upon whatever excuse it is waged, is always the effect of a sudden insight into the true nature of the world and man. Life is something which should never have been; and so in fiery moments of intelligence we kill each other." [7] And he predicts in 1905 that because of competing empires, great things will happen: "the world will yet know greater men that Caesar and Napoleon, deeper passion and wider humanity than Shakespeare's, a music still more elemental than Wagner's, a sadder soul than Schopenhauer's, a more triumphant intellect than Nietzsche's, beauty more enthralling than Helen's; . . . The world is barely adolescent, and . . . its majority cannot be until after a thousand years of war between the East and the West, when the yellow man and the white man have fought it out on equal terms, and learnt which is master." [8] Quite clearly Davidson considers war to be part of the evolutionary process; he hopes war will evoke bigger and better and more heroic things from humanity. In any case, war does not seem distasteful to him; rather, it seems that he looks forward to this great conflict with some anticipation. Cramb's Darwinistic explanation of the historical process is undoubtedly in the background of Davidson's prophecy of war.

Not only does Davidson write poetry about empire, but he argues that poetry and empire are directly related. In *The Theatrocrat*, for example, the Bishop of St. James's attributes the great burst of English drama during the Renaissance at least in part to the expansion of the British Empire. Presumably, Edwardian England, now that she is expanding her empire, will once again breed great poetry. No doubt Davidson as the poet of empire hopes to be a precursor of that great poetry, or perhaps he regards his own poetry as the first of the new great tradition.

More specifically, English expansion and exploration during the sixteenth century brought forth what Davidson considers the world's greatest verse form, blank verse. In the "Ode on the Coronation" he says that blank verse, "England's lordly measure," evolved during the Renaissance when man's "profound insatiate soul" needed "a deep-toned, more material song." [9] Thus, blank verse is not only matter's most noble means of expression, as I noted in Chapter 5, but it originated when a people were doing what Davidson says all people should be doing—striving for mastery. In fact, he says, "poetry is the will to live and the will to power; poetry is the empire. Poetry is life and force; and England, being most amply replenished with the will to live and the will to power, possesses in her blank verse the greatest poetry in the world." [10] Poetry emanates from the same psychological forces as empire; therefore, poetry does not just praise empire: "Poetry is empire." Davidson's "expressive theory" seems to assume that all human actions—poetry or war—arise from the wish to mastery. Just as English superiority is reflected in a superior verse form, superiority of the English as world rulers is reflected in the empire.

Not surprisingly, as a corollary to these ideas, Davidson disparages other nations and other races. For example, he denies that all humanity has a common ancestor in some aboriginal man: "the white man, the black man, the red man, and the yellow man had not a common origin any more than a common language. Matter always recalled in its unconscious memory what it had done, and improved on past attempts." [11] The implication is that the white race is matter's most successful achievement; and, if there is any doubt about it, Davidson is unequivocal in the introduction to *The Theatrocrat*. "It is certain that Matter has not evolved a finer race of men than the Caucasians," he writes, and having thus said he specifically discusses the English: "It is certain that the Caucasian has not evolved a finer breed than the Greeks, the Romans, or the English." [12] And Davidson's empire builder relegated to the hell of the dominated "The greater part/ Of all the swarthy all the tawny tribes." [13] Obviously, the black and yellow peoples are fit only to be ruled. In Davidson's English heaven of masters, there is little room for anyone but the white man. Although to us imperialism seems not only outmoded but unethical, to Davidson extension of empire is justifiable. Davidson had taken to attacking Christian ethics, and after 1905 he attacked Christianity more often, more ardently, and on wider grounds.

### III   *Heroism and Empire: Democracy and Christianity*

Davidson was fully cognizant of the antithesis between his heroic philosophy and Christian ethics, and he was by no means apologetic about it. In fact, he often said that Christianity is the cause of the world's problems, the problems which he thought he could solve. But, if Christianity is opposed to his materialism, there are also many conflicts between his heroism and Christianity. If men must have a God, says Davidson, let him be one that is worthy of a materialistic, empire-building nation. In *The Testament of a Prime Minister*,[14] the heroic prime minister muses that what imperial England needs is not a Hebrew God:

> Shall we not now observantly dethrone
> The valetudinary God of woe,
> The foreign God that died a shameful death,
> ...................................................................
> Exalt instead the nerve, the brain, the blood
> The power of us, victorious Englishmen . . . ?
> (73–74)

Obviously, he does not care for Jesus, whose obedience caused him to suffer and die. He prefers a Teutonic god of strength; or, perhaps, one of England's own making; in short, he wants a god made in the image of a Davidsonian English hero.

The prime minister then has his vision of the death of God and sin, which is followed by a vision of the judgment before the great white throne of the Davidsonian god. Entering into the joys of salvation are "the great ones of the earth . . ./ The kings, the conquerors, the wise, the bold/ The rich, the proud" (83). But cast into the eternal fires of hell are "the Son of Man and His elect," the poor in spirit, and those who hungered after righteousness (85). Davidson's heaven, we remember from *The Empire-Builder*, is "here and now." If man is to achieve his rewards in this life, he cannot get them by behaving like a Christian. Empires, personal or political, are not built by the truly merciful and meek but by those who enjoy "their power and pleasure in the world" (83).

Thus at the heart of Davidson's dislike for Christian morality is an attack on Christian love. Such a morality, says Davidson, is for slaves, not for the masters that the English are fated to be. And to his mind the Christian "slave-morality" is directly related to democracy and socialism, both of which he regards as part of a decadence which he frequently satirizes and criticizes.[15] Ostensibly, decadence is the object of Davidson's attack; and Christian love applied to politics, which means socialism to him, is a mark of decadence. "Socialism is the final stage in the decadence of Christendom," and it will corrupt "the whole body of the State" if allowed to flourish.[16] And again, "The enemy of man is Socialism in all its forms: Socialism is decadence, is death." [17]

Decadence, we must surmise, is Davidson's word for Christian charity, meekness, and remorse of conscience. It is the opposite of heroism, he believes, in that it negates and rejects life while vitalism affirms and embraces life. In the 1890's, he attacked ennui and boredom and the repression of natural desires as being decadent (*Earl Lavender*); but now he shifts the focus of his attack to the Christ-like characteristics of mercy and mildness, peacemaking and long-suffering. In short, he must disparage those social, political, and ethical ideals which conflict with the extreme self-expression of hero worship and political expansionism. As a result of these views he must destroy both democratic socialism and Christianity in order that his new system might be imposed: "Socialism is the decadence of Feudalism; that is to say, it is less than nothing. At its very utmost it is only a bad smell; rejoicing in itself very much at present, as bad smells are wont to do: Europe is noisome with it. Feudalism, Christendom, Socialism, cannot be changed. What we have to do is to leave it all; . . . and come out into the Universe." [18]

This very strong statement against Christianity and socialism clearly indicates that the break with Christianity is complete. During his early and middle years, he had openly attacked the orthodox creeds of Christianity; now he openly attacks Christian ethics, both on the grounds of his materialism and of his heroic vitalism. The relationship of Davidson's ideas to Nietzsche's seems indisputable; for, as John A. Lester indicates, "It was largely Nietzsche who taught Davidson to regard Christianity as the prime cause of the degeneracy of modern man." In his youth, Lester notes, Davidson had resented the creeds, but his reading of Nietzsche gave him the conviction that Christendom "had sickened men with life, so that priests might rule." Lester notes that, significantly, both Davidson and Nietzsche say that there had been only one Christian and that he died on the cross. Both of them believe that, since Christ's death, Christianity "has lain like an incubus over Western Europe, sickening mankind with remorse, blinding man to his instincts, and ever the foe of life." [19]

Nevertheless, we must remember that Davidson attacked both the deeds and the creeds of Christianity. Davidson presumably thought that his heroism undermined Christian ethics, while his materialism undermined Christian theology. Davidson makes his new god the striving of matter for self-expression; the law of life is strife, not love; and the basis of being is not that God is love but that God is heroic egoism. In the Mammon plays the destruction of Christianity is, as we have noted, the theme; and Davidson's protagonist lives the new ethics and the new theology of materialism and vitalism.

## IV  *The Relationships Between Heroic Vitalism and Materialism*

So far, we have traced two separate themes in Davidson's writings. We have noted that, during the last years of his life, he finds an answer—scientific materialism— to the problems of belief which have troubled him through much of his career. We have also observed that Davidson's admiration for heroic behavior changes to hero worship and finally to a gospel of strength. In the works of his last years—the Mammon plays and *The Testament of John Davidson*—the two themes merge fully. At first glance, the two ideas, materialism and vitalism, seem completely antithetical. Materialim implies mechanism and determinism, while heroic vitalism stresses free will and mastery over circumstances. However, Davidson assigns to matter a certain amount of self-will; for, to Davidson, matter has an unconscious drive toward self-knowledge which has culminated in man. His materialism is "creative," and it bears relationships to the sort of creative evolution set forth by Samuel Butler and G. B. Shaw. Man may utilize and control this drive since he is creative matter become self-conscious. Thus Davidson's materialism ("a new poetry") is presumably not mechanistic. Nevertheless, most of the relationships between Davidson's materialism and vitalism are on a level which we might describe as pragmatic, not theoretical.

As we have seen, becoming a materialist means for Davidson destroying Christianity, not only Christian theology, but also Christian ethics. For the true materialist lives "in the Universe," and this means partaking in the amorality of the universe. Being thus in harmony with the universe, which consists of matter striving toward self-realization, the materialist must drop the Christian ethic of humility and meekness and join the battle for self-fulfillment. For Davidson, the true nature of things, the ground of our being (as Paul Tillich would say), is not love but competition. To recognize this fact is to behave like a Davidsonian hero.

In another practical sense, the propagation of the gospel of materialism demands heroic efforts. As Davidson explains it, he himself has to be a hero: "All poets are fanatics. No poet ever wrote a line that lives who was not willing to die for his figure of speech, his melody, his vision. I am a propagandist. All poets worthy of the name were and are propagandists, their aim being to extend their self-consciousness into the self-consciousness of the world until the ear and sight of all men live in their melody and vision." [20] The duty of the poet-hero, he says, is nothing less than preparing the world for the message of materialism, persuading it to come out into the universe and its amorality, and developing "an actual conception of the Universe in which the mind and imagination of men, homeless since God and Sin and Heaven and

Hell ceased to be vital, must find a new abiding-place. I would cast away the dreams, the lore, the rags, the rust of thirty centuries. . . . ." [21] In short, the great work of informing mankind of its materialistic origins and of setting it free from the restraints of Christianity can be carried out only by a superhero who has rid himself of the Christian (and sometimes Socialist) vices of pity, fear, and kindness toward his fellow man.[22] A full dramatization of this materialist-hero is to be found in Davidson's last two plays.

## V  *The Hero as Materialist: The "God and Mammon" Plays*

"In my book, 'The Theatrocrat,'" Davidson writes in 1905, "I lead the way out of Christendom. I take the first resolute step out of Christendom. What is beyond I cannot rightly see as yet, but I will see, and it will be better than Christendom. . . ." [23] The Mammon plays portray what is beyond: "For half a century I have survived in a world entirely unfitted for me, and having known both the Heaven and the Hell thereof, and being without a revenue and an army and navy to compel the nations, I begin definitely in my Testaments and Tragedies to destroy this unfit world and make it over again in my image. . . ." [24] The Mammon plays, more so than the Testaments, are a dramatization, first, of a hero's destroying the unfit world of Christianity, and, second, of the world which the hero would like to create to replace the old one. These plays, are, therefore, a kind of practical exercise in revaluation. They show us Davidson's message put into practice; they show us what is beyond Christendom—the picture is not pleasant.

*The Triumph of Mammon,* completed in February, 1907, and published on Davidson's fiftieth birthday, April 11, 1907, is the first part of a projected series of plays to be called "God and Mammon: A Trilogy." [25] Only two of the three plays were completed. Although he does not say so, Davidson has no doubt by this time abandoned any hopes he may have had for getting his thesis plays produced. This play is intended, therefore, not for the stage but for the reader.[26]

As the play begins, two ships are entering the harbor of Christianstadt, the principal city of the kingdom of Thule, a modern European nation that is symbolically any modern Christian nation. From one of the ships comes Guendolen, Princess of the Isles, who has come to marry Prince Magnus, second son of King Christian of Thule. The other ship carries Mammon, the elder son of King

Christian, who three years before had been exiled from Thule for having blasphemed God at his wedding ceremony. He was to have married Guendolen; but, because of his actions, the ceremony was not completed. His name was changed from Christian to Mammon, and he was told to return to Christianstadt only if he were penitent. But he returns impenitent, "a man apart" (19), the Man Forbid, demanding to see the king.

Magnus and Guendolen, who are both Christians and hence merciful and long-suffering, agree to let Mammon have an audience with old King Christian. However, in order to fulfill the King's command, Mammon must be clothed in sackcloth and have a rope around his neck. Magnus and Guendolen hope that in thus forcing Mammon to confront his father, dressed as a penitent, even as hard a man as Mammon might be softened. And thereby hangs the central scene of the play.

King Christian rejoices over the repentance and return of his prodigal son; like the prodigal's father, he declares that "this my son/ Was dead and is alive again" (39). Though he is "baresark and haltered," Mammon is by no means contrite: "No Christian; Mammon, I" (39). Indeed, he announces that "My title, Mammon,/ Delights me: I shall make this name renowned/ For things unprecedented through the earth" (43). His Nietzschean (and Davidsonian) attack on Christianity blames it for the world's ennui, and he declares defiantly that he came back for two reasons: to impregnate Guendolen and to seize the throne of Thule. By the first act, he will show his disdain for Christian morality and express the inherent amorality of the universe; by the second, he will finally destroy the kingdom of God and set up the kingdom of Mammon.

Mammon's brother Magnus, behaving more like Davidson's heroes than a Christian, wants Mammon put to death; but King Christian, unwilling to kill a soul unsaved, will not allow it. The Abbot Gottlieb, who speaks for orthodox Christianity in the play, remembers an old statute and recommends a better punishment, one which will put a stop to Mammon's designs on Guendolen— castration. Furthermore, according to another old law, no eunuch may be king of Thule; thus Mammon's plans might be effectively crippled. Guendolen, who still feels attracted to Mammon, wants to be married to Magnus immediately to forestall any attempt Mammon might make on her. The abbot agrees to do it.

Meanwhile, Mammon continues to strike at Christianity. Castration, he says, is just what Christianity demands:

> Unsex us all, the final blessed state
> Of Christendom: geld, spay them, men and women,
> And start on earth your pallid Heaven of neuters
> Where marriage is not!
>
> (52)

The supposed sexlessness of Christianity is symbolic of its rejection of life and of its failure to be in harmony with an amoral, vitalistic universe.

The central scene of the play (Act III, Scene 2) finds Mammon in the palace chapel, bound to a pillar face to face with a large crucifix, and condemned to be castrated by his father, King Christian. In a long soliloquy (63–66), Mammon again quarrels with Christianity for its decadence. King Christian comes to perform the castration, which he says is a symbolic act, like Abraham's sacrifice of Isaac in ancient times, or like God's sacrifice of His son on the cross. Knife in hand, Christian tells Mammon that Guendolen is now married to Magnus. Just as Christian is about to make the sacrifice, Mammon relents and cries, "God help me then! Christ save me! . . . Oh father, I repent" (73). When Christian cuts Mammon's bonds and lays down the knife, Mammon seizes it, stabs the king three times, and cries out, "I would you were the soul of Christendom!/ I would you had been God!" (75).

Telling his guard, Oswald, that King Christian killed himself in a mad fit, Mammon commandeers the armed forces of Thule with Oswald's help, and he promises a bloodbath if he is thwarted again:

> Ten thousand old, conceited Christian dolts,
> Amazed by death, shall in their life-blood bathe,
> Or ever I forgo one swelling pulse,
> One sumptuous tide of my superb desire.
>
> (76)

At the hour of midnight he and Oswald set off to find the bridal suite of Guendolen and Magnus, for Mammon plans to kill them both. In the next scene, Guendolen refuses to consummate the

marriage to Magnus because she finds the sex act beastly and un-
clean. She has an idea that she might have another immaculate
conception:

> Some still night,
> Together lying in each other's arms,
> I thought my passive soul entwined with yours
> Would once again conceive the Son of Man.
>
> .................................................................
>
> To be a wife is sin, since God's own son
> Was first conceived by tidings, not by marriage.
> (82–83)

Obviously, Davidson is arguing that Christianity perverts man's
natural passions, destroys his will, prevents him from enjoying
that most normal means of self-assertiveness, the sex drive, and
turns into sin what should be his greatest joy. As symbolized by
Guendolen, Christianity is sterile, even denying the procreation of
life.

Just after Guendolen has admitted to Magnus that she has felt
sexual desire—for Mammon—Mammon bursts into the bridal
chamber. He keeps Guendolen occupied with looking out the window at the moon while he grapples with Magnus and pushes him
into the hallway, where he falls on the poised swords of Mammon's troops and dies: an "accident," says Mammon (88).

Then Mammon sets about to finish the job, to kill Guendolen
as well; for, though he loves her, he does not want her after
Magnus has already possessed her body. When she protests her
virginity, he changes his mind, orders her into bed, and proceeds
to preach her a sermon on matter. He goes through the gospel of
matter, point by point, explaining to her that there is no God, sin,
or afterlife, but that there is "the Universe." To realize that she is
the universe is "to be a star," he tells her; she is made of the same
matter as the stars in the heavens (95). In the same metaphor,
even coition is the collision of two stars. Such materialistic logic
and atomic imagery overwhelm Guendolen; she immediately becomes a convert to Davidsonian materialism and, of course, readily yields herself to Mammon, forgetting all of her fastidiousness
about the supposed beastiliness of sexual intercourse. As the scene
ends, Mammon is about to make love to Guendolen, amid a great
flurry of pseudoscientific talk, star colliding with star, "rich gal-

axies of soul" leaping from his veins, "to hide their fires in the
sweet heaven" of Guendolen (99).

Thus, in *The Triumph of Mammon,* Mammon has conquered
by killing King Christian and Magnus and by seducing Guendolen. This allegorical action of the play is loaded with Christian
diction and images. King Christian is God, thus also representative
of the power of God in the world. Mammon is a son of God, a
Satan or a rebel Jesus, who takes upon him the sins of the world
and likes them. Mammon also stands for mankind, especially that
part of mankind's nature which strives for self-fulfillment in this
world and which serves itself, not God. Magnus is another Son of
God, more like the traditional Jesus Christ; and, until the triumph
of Mammon, Magnus is the heir to the throne, a sort of viceregent
of God. Guendolen is in one sense representative of the Virgin
Mary, since she desires another virgin birth; but, more importantly, she is the church in the world, the mystical bride of Christ.
Christian and Magnus *head* the church; Guendolen *is* the church.
Her marriage to Magnus suggests the relationship between the
church and the Christ, the Son of God, while her admitted desire
for Mammon indicates that the church in the world is only too
subject to the temptations of the flesh.

In murdering Magnus, Mammon has symbolically destroyed
Jesus, whose ministry as portrayed in the Gospels gave rise to the
Christian ideal of love, meekness, and humility. This ethic of self-
effacement is in conflict with Davidson's heroic vitalism, and the
killing of Magnus represents the triumph of a Nietzschean master
morality over the Christian slave morality, Davidson's philosophy
of the amorality of the universe over Christian ideas of right and
wrong. It is the death of sin.

Mammon's triumph is completed when he seduces Guendolen,
the bride of Magnus-Christ. The ideas of God and Jesus being
dead, Guendolen, the church in the world and the ordinary Christian, gets over her notions about the evils of fleshly desires, accepts
Mammon's vitalism and materialism, comes out into the universe
and immediately gains new satisfactions as the handmaiden of the
heroic character Mammon. Therefore, Christian theology and
Christian ethics are inverted and destroyed: Magnus-Jesus dies in
order that man might be free to sin, that man might know that Sin
is the very essence of the universe. Theoretically, the triumph of
Mammon is complete; but Davidson knew that in reality he was a

long way from triumph. So he wrote another act to this play, and another play besides.

Mammon is a pragmatist: though he may have symbolically brought down Christianity and started the world over again, he has by no means established the kingdom of matter. As Act V begins, he is holding court, interviewing suppliants, and trying to decide whom he may use in his bid for power. He expects conflict: "There shall be deeper depths of poverty,/ A more distressing toil, more warlike war . . ." (116). He is frankly worried about whether or not he will be able to succeed with the revaluation.

In the second scene of the last act, Mammon plans to confront an audience of the people of Thule at St. Olaf's Hall, where he has placed the bodies of Christian and Magnus. It is the day after the murders. Before he arrives, the Abbot Gottlieb takes the situation in hand and makes a "friends, Romans, countrymen" speech, using the exposed bodies as his visual aids, and accusing Mammon of murder.

Mammon retorts with a series of lies: his father killed himself, and he claims that he and Magnus were snarled in some kind of conspiracy to seize the throne. The crowd demands that Mammon take the ancient test of innocence by touching the wounds. In going toward the bodies, he trips and falls against the catafalque upon which the bodies lie; and, according to one of the onlookers, the wounds bleed. Meanwhile, the papal legate, Anselm, ascending the catafalque, asserts the temporal authority of the Catholic Church by excommunicating Mammon and by leading a large part of the crowd with him out of the hall. As they go, they chant "Deliver me, O God, from the evil man" (138), and the stage direction tells us that the chant continues uninterrupted outside.

Suddenly "a noise of tumult breaks out" offstage; a mob is forming. Immediately, at Mammon's order, "the shattering repercussive fire of a machine gun is heard, accompanied by a great outcry, and succeeded by profound silence" (139). Mammon's promised bloodbath has begun; or, as he describes it,

> The crash of blood! a cataract of blood!
> Upon the pavement plunging! Secular change
> At every period is sprinkled so;
> Nor could the portal of the world I make
> Escape the crimson baptism.

In short, if men want change, they must spill blood. To be baptized into Davidson's new creation, the world must suffer.

The mob disperses, and the soldiers, together with those who remain in the hall, shout "Long live the King." Whereupon Mammon launches into a sermon on materialism (the second in this play) which lasts for 121 lines. At the end of his tirade, he has attained a measure of success; as the stage direction puts it, "The older people regard each other dubiously; but the soldiers and the young folk raise a great shout as the curtain falls" (145).

Meanwhile, at the palace Guendolen awaits Mammon. Hearing the machine-gun fire, she asks her maid Prounice what it was, and her response to Prounice's answer may be taken as an indication of the difference between Guendolen, the squeamish Christian who found the sex act beastly, and Guendolen, the heroic materialist. Some are injured and some are dead, Prounice tells her as she sits at the piano. Prounice suggests to her that she might ask the King about it when he comes, but she replies that "unless he speaks of it, I shall not ask" (145). And that is the end of her concern about the machine-gunning of her subjects. It presumably illustrates how "anything is better than Christendom."

When Mammon arrives, she says no more about it; instead, she tells him that she has conceived. Thus the symbolic joining together of Mammon and the Church personified in Guendolen is already bearing fruit, in contrast to the barrenness of the union of Magnus-Christ and Guendolen.

In *The Triumph of Mammon,* Davidson dramatizes a hero who is a materialist, a believer in the creeds of matter and of Davidsonian heroism, something very like a Nietzschean Overman. He takes what are supposed to be heroic measures to destroy old values, chiefly Christian values, in order to bring about the ultimate revaluation. The ideas of God, Jesus, and sin are dead; the rule of Mammon, the evil one, is set up; and Mammon easily seduces the church when Christ dies permanently. Clearly, for Mammon (and for Davidson) the end justifies the means; in the conflict that must inevitably arise between new and old, Mammon and Christian, anything is permitted, whether it be out-and-out lying or coldblooded machine-gunning. If Mammon begins to look like a twentieth-century dictator, from either the far right or the far left, it is no surprise, for his philosophy and his method are of a pattern which by mid-century we all recognize. *Mammon and His Message* will make the point perfectly clear.

In *Mammon and His Message*,[27] the second part of the projected "God and Mammon" trilogy, Davidson shows Mammon acting "heroically" to secure his hold upon the throne of Thule. The action follows that of *The Triumph of Mammon* by a week, "the time having been employed by Mammon in the mobilization of the army of Thule, and its cantonment in and about Christianstadt" (xiv). In the opening scene, Anselm, the papal legate in Thule, is reprimanding Guendolen for living in sin with Mammon. She advises him to forget about morality, to leave Christianity, and to join her in the religion of matter. Though Anselm is almost persuaded, he leaves holding to Christianity.

Meanwhile, Mammon discusses the affairs of Thule with his chancellor, Florimond. The city of Christianstadt is in the hands of Mammon's loyal army:

> ... I took
> My army in my fist to batter down
> The churches, scourge the Christians hence and carve
> The world in my own image. ...
>
> (16)

He has assumed personal, dictatorial control of the whole of Thule; his methods are, as we have noted, uncomfortably totalitarian. In *The Triumph of Mammon*, he took control of the press, told outright lies, and machine-gunned a mob; [28] now, in *Mammon and His Message*, Davidson is plainly saying again and again that the end justifies the means: might means right. Though the people of Thule wish to leave, Mammon has stopped emigration (17). He plans to put to use an ancient rack which is kept in Christianstadt as a tourist attraction (18–19), and he engages in a neat bit of doublethink: "To shed blood is to cleanse" (20). How does he justify his actions? "The laxity that marred my father's reign/ I've medicine for" (17). Besides, he argues, the hero may follow his intuitions no matter where they lead him: "Men may do what they list without a thought" (19).

The amoral Mammon, however, having that curious brand of puritanism one finds among revolutionaries (for example, Robespierre), wants his subjects to be moral. Being completely immoral in public matters, he compensates by insisting upon an almost pietistically rigorous morality about sexual matters. Mammon begins by trying to reform the prostitutes, whom he of course blames on Christianity (27). He offers them a choice: cash payments to those who marry and live with a husband; death to those who continue in prostitution.

After the harlots, he focuses his attention on a crowd of old beggars and criminals of both sexes, whom Mammon calls "the very proper offal of Christendom." He will not abide them, he says:

> I'll not have
> The pauper with me always, hatefullest
> Legacy of Christ. I'll have no poor at all;
> And no incurables, no criminals,
> No bedlamites. I'll cut out all that's Christ;
> And down shall come asylums, hospitals,
> With churches, colleges, and culture-marts;
> I'll raze out cities and dilapidate
> The structure of society to lay
> The ghost of Christendom.
>
> (36–37)

"I'll purge the world of you," he raves (38). He will poison them and, with them, all the impotent men and women past conception.

Davidson's ideas expressed in this scene might well be compared with Ninian's statement in the eclogue "Lammas," discussed in Chapter 4. Ninian condemns Christianity for having made

> A merit of defect, a cult of woe,
> Sowing exhausted land with seed that's foul,
> To harvest tares of madness, impotence,
> Uncomeliness in wasteful granaries—
> I mean asylums, prisons, hospitals.[29]

If a "gospel of the pride of life," or in other words, a gospel of heroic vitalism, had been instituted instead of the Christian gospel,

> How had the world
> Approved the excellent expedient,
> With voluntary euthanasia
> Weeded humanity at once, and made
> A race of heroes in a golden age . . . !"[30]

As observed in Chapter 4, this idea is presented in "Lammas" from behind an ironic mask, so that we cannot say that the idea has Davidson's approval. After all, the speaker is Ninian (Ninny). But, as also pointed out in Chapter 4, certain ideas about which Davidson retains ironic noncommittal during the 1890's have a way of appearing in the later works in contexts where there can be no doubt of Davidson's approval. This idea is one good example. Ninian's "voluntary euthanasia" becomes involuntary euthanasia in the kingdom of Mammon.[31]

Like the Man Forbid, Mammon wishes to obliterate the traces of humanistic and Christian culture; he will tear down "colleges and culture marts" (37). He would presumably substitute for humane learning an education in matter, like that recommended by Davidson in 1905:

This is a great part of my immorality, that, instead of a myth, children should be told, as soon as they begin to express their wonder, that they consist of oxygen, hydrogen, nitrogen, carbon, calcium, kalium, natrium, sulphur, phosphorus, iron, magnesium, silicon; that the principal human elements are also the principal constituents of the whole Universe, and that all the elements are forms of one substance. They should also be shown experimentally the qualities and properties of these elements; and gradually, instead of catechisms and the grammars of dead languages, obtain a knowledge of the poetry of evolution: a poetry that does not require to be taught or learnt; that requires only to be told and shown to be known, welcomed, and remembered, because it is already subconscious in the Matter of which we consist.[32]

This theory implies that ideas are innate; education would be simply a task of awakening in the student the ideas that are inherent because of his materiality. Mammon is a man who has become in this sense educated; he is matter become fully self-conscious, as Davidson puts it.

Like a typical dictator, Mammon takes the law as well as the army and the press into his hands. With the papal legate Anselm and the Abbot Gottlieb imprisoned, Florimond warns Mammon that "not only Thule, but Europe calls for justice." I have my army firmly in hand, says Mammon, "and now intend/ Such justice as omnipotence may deal" (41). To show the effects of an ideology in which the end justifies the means, we might compare Mammon's actions with thoughts Davidson expressed about imprisonment three years before in 1905, at a time when he had just served on a jury: "A way out of prison must be found, and shortly. I hope that fifty years hence men will look back on imprisonment and its unmentionable horror and shame with a greater loathing than that with which we today regard the thumbscrew and the rack." [33] Yet Mammon's message is Davidson's, and Mammon's methods are Davidson's. And we must suppose that we are seeing evidence of what it means to "come out of Christianity."

After confronting the Jesuit Anselm unsuccessfully with his gospel, Mammon tries to convert him by force: "Say after me 'Get thee behind me, God;/ I follow Mammon.' Say it, say it!" (57). But Anselm will not, of course; Mammon throws the old man down violently and kills him. This murder is too much even for Mammon, and he has a hallucination in which three bodies are lying on the floor, their wounds seemingly writhing and sucking the air (59), no doubt representing the three men he has murdered.

In the following scene, Mammon, talking with the commander of his army, Oswald, counsels him not to delay marrying his fiancée, Inga the Volsung, whose name suggests something of her Wagnerian and supposedly heroic female nature. When Oswald is ordered to torture Abbot Gottlieb on the rack, he wants to back out, but Mammon says no; Oswald is too human, too Christ-like. He needs discipline. As he recounts to Oswald how he murdered his father and brother, Mammon has another vision of their bodies, which terrifies even the great Mammon. As Townsend says, Oswald may be taken to represent Mammon's conscience; [34] he is, in a sense, Davidson's alter ego, the Davidson who in 1905 criticized the horror of the prison and looked upon it as a terrible anachronism, as loathsome as the thumbscrew and the rack. Mammon's hallucinations also reflect this side of Davidson, who no doubt recognized in himself much of the softness and humaneness of the Christian conscience; his Christianity kept getting the better of him. In forcing Oswald to torture Gottlieb, Davidson is symbolically suppressing his own unheroic characteristics of mercy and kindness (recall the poems of social criticism). He is trying, therefore, to effect the triumph of Mammon over John Davidson as well as over Christianity.

Although Mammon advises Oswald to marry Inga, Inga, it appears, would rather have Mammon. She comes to him at the palace

from her house in Watling Street, looking for a heroic mate (82).
After Mammon gives her a short heroic lecture, she immediately
yields to him. Inga, who follows her instincts by coming of her
own will to the palace to find Mammon, is a female Davidson
hero. She comes from her house in Watling Street, which suggests
that she already lives in the Universe, and she is presumably in
harmony with nature even before she meets Mammon. Unlike
Guendolen, she does not need to be converted from corrupt Christianity before she can unite with Mammon. Like Mammon, she
accepts her intuitions and emotions as the best guide to behavior;
and her feelings are heroic in the Davidson sense.

Having seduced Inga, Mammon goes immediately to the torture
chamber where he and Oswald prepare to put Gottlieb upon the
rack, in spite of Oswald's objections. For, as Mammon says, "that
which we do with all our might is just" (90). Furthermore, he
burns the abbey of Christianstadt, another symbolic strike against
Christianity. Although Guendolen does not like seeing the Gothic
abbey destroyed, she finally agrees it is best that "not a Christian
shard be left on earth." Nothing is too extreme to bring about the
revaluation, Mammon insists,

> To purge the world of Christianity
> The sacrifice of every human life
> That now enjoys or nauseates the sun,
> Would not be too exorbitant a price.
> (103)

Of course, that price does not include Mammon and Guendolen.
Like Adam and Eve, they would then be "in Eden left alone," to
create an earthly paradise from which God could not exile them
since the ideas of God and sin are dead. Paradise would be re-
gained.

The play concludes with a long scene in St. Olaf's Square in
Christianstadt. Mammon learns that he is out of money, and in his
need he curses Christianity again: "Money is Christendom!" he
cries (126). The mob, stirred up and after him, cry that he is an
incendiary, murderer, parricide, assassin, and torturer. Worse yet,
Oswald has defected and is trying, with some success, to turn the
people against King Mammon. But Mammon retains control of the
army; he sends one force to rob the bank of Thule and another to
aim artillery at the house where Oswald is hiding out.

From the window of the Palace of Thule, Mammon advises the crowd to adopt his slogan, "Get thee behind me, God; I follow Mammon" (136). We learn that the bank has fallen to Mammon and that Oswald and the other malcontents have been routed. As the scene draws to a close, "the opening bars of a heroic march are heard, and at the same time the walls of the abbey fall in." Mammon's comment is a fitting summary of the final scenes:

> So all the bastions of Christendom
> Shall crumble into dust.—Begin again:
> Your clangourous trumpets—let them peal it out;
> Your cymbals, and the thunder of your drums!
> (140)

The play ends, but the conflict will not end for some time, for Mammon pledges to continue his reign of terror until all vestiges of the old value system are wiped out.

What, then, is the "message" of *Mammon and His Message*? It is, of course, the gospel of matter and heroism; but it is also Davidson's special pragmatic message portrayed in the action of the play: he wants to explain to the public how a hero would destroy this unfit world and make it over again in his own image. As Mammon seduces Inga the Volsung, he declares "My message is a deed, always a deed" (86). And Mammon's deeds we have seen. He has stopped freedom of expression, upset the processes of law, pledged to destroy the weak and the impotent, tortured an old man, wrecked the symbols of Christianity, taken over the country by military might. It is difficult to believe that Davidson means what he says; but he evidently does, though he realizes that we will wonder.

"Is this the thing I want to say?" he asks in the Epilogue to *Mammon and Mis Message*. "Is this the thing that should be said? . . ."

I say the thing I want to say, recognizing enmity as the sign of my success and the unintended warrant of my power and authority. I say the thing I want to say and immediately thought is wounded, ideas are in the crucible, idols are overturned. . . .

I must be certain only that the thing I say is the thing I mean; and being man, and not a creed, or a party, or a culture, I will then say that which should be said, because man is the Universe become conscious. . . . We must make ourselves so well understood that men, compelled to misunderstand us in self-defence, will maintain that it is an allegory, that it is symbol, that we do not mean it. . . .

I devour, digest, and assimilate the Universe; make for myself in my Testaments and Tragedies a new form and substance of Imagination; and by poetic power certify the semi-certitudes of science.[35]

In short, Davidson clearly intended that the Mammon plays should dramatize a Davidsonian hero in action. The hero symbolically destroys Christianity and establishes a Nietzschean rule of strength—he is an overman in action. He believes in himself; above all, he believes that might means right and practices what he preaches. In fact, in practice this hero is a prototype of the twentieth-century dictator: Hitler, Mussolini, Stalin, or several others. What Davidson wanted was a complete revaluation of all values, the replacement of the ideas and ideals of agape and Christian love with an ethic of self-realization. Mammon objectifies Davidson's conception of the ethic of heroic vitalism as it would be practiced by a materialist. Mammon is something more (or less) than a persona; he is a mouthpiece for Davidson's ideas, a puppet performing Davidson's symbolic actions, a self-portrait. He is very nearly Davidson himself, projected into a story about an exiled prince of Thule who takes over the country.

This identification of poet and persona is the plays' most notable weakness as well as being perhaps the source of their strength. On the one hand, they are too clearly thesis plays to have any credence; they represent neither an imitation of nature nor a subjective perception of the universe colored by the imagination or creativeness of the poet. They are plainly dramatizations of Davidson's system, with characters rising not out of human experience but out of Davidson's dreams of heroes; and the action comes not from conflicts of recognizable or even metaphorically representative characters but from Davidson's manipulation of reality for propaganda purposes, Or, to put it another way, we read Davidson's plays (or theoretically go to see Davidson's plays) not to see how the story will end, but to study the development of his ideas.

But, on the other hand, the Mammon plays do have their own excitement—a kind of urgency and force which makes one keep reading. No doubt this strength comes because the plays are so intensely personal, because in some sense Mammon is John Davidson. The reader is fascinated with a poet so supremely confident in the rightness of his opinions as to wish to force the whole world into his mold. And, having come from a time when many writers were entirely swept up in the mode of "art for art's sake," a moralist like Davidson demands our attention by his fierce determination, whether we sympathize with his moralizing or not.

## VI   *The Hero as John Davidson:* The Testament of John Davidson

In the last poem Davidson published before he committed suicide, he abandoned all pretenses of esthetic distance and detachment between himself and his persona and called the hero by his own name. John Davidson is the hero of *The Testament,* but its action is symbolic: it does not chronicle actual events in Davidson's life. The poem again portrays a materialistic hero, this time named John Davidson, who vanquishes immaterial forces. The difference between this and the other testaments is that Davidson admits that his ideas are to be identified with the hero's. He hides behind no mask. The resulting poem is *The Testament of John Davidson,* published in 1908,[36] the longest and most complex of the five testaments, a "minor epic," Townsend calls it,[37] perhaps with more implied praise than the poem deserves. Placed between what Davidson calls "a poem of the dawn of life and a poem of its close" (32), *The Testament of John Davidson* is thus ironically juxtaposed to one poem of tempered optimism, "Honeymoon," and one poem of stoic resignation, "The Last Journey."

Besides the Testament, the volume contains a lengthy prose dedication, a verse prologue, and an epilogue. The dedication, addressed boldly to "The Peers Temporal of the United Kingdoms of Great Britain and Ireland" (11), is an attempt by Davidson to enlist the aid of the English aristocracy in his struggle to replace Christendom with the kingdom of Mammon. He assumes that they must feel strongly the effects of the decadence in the attrition of their power. Half-seriously, half-facetiously, he advises the lords to ignore the demands of women, of the Irish, and of labor, and to come out into the universe. The women do not need suffrage; the Irish can take care of themselves; and labor need only be reminded to get busy and make use of its native ability to succeed. "You have heard of the Overman?" he asks rhetorically. Well, no need for an evolutionary Overman in England, for "the Englishman is the Overman; and the history of England is the history of his evolution" (17–18).

*The Testament of John Davidson* takes up where *The Man Forbid* left off. When suddenly the world was closed to him, he writes, he built a "palace in the Milky Way," which is one way of expressing his "coming out into the universe," as he puts it in other places.

Feeling the loss of energy and of sensory perceptions, Davidson decides to return from his "palace in the Milky Way" to earth to die; like his heroes Smith, Hallowes, and Ninian, he believes that "exempt from death is he who takes his life" (46). He is practicing his own recommended voluntary euthanasia. However, when he realizes that, if he dies, "the Universe shall cease/ To know itself," he decides not to take his life after all. Thus refreshed, he finds his energy renewed and experience rich again (50).

No sooner does he come back to life than he hears a sound which he correctly interprets as divinity approaching. Having killed many gods in battle, he assumes that some deity, adamant and armed with thunder, seeks revenge. Davidson prepares for heroic action as the god comes nearer. However, it is a goddess, not a god; it is Diana, attired very appealingly in a green simarre, driving her chariot drawn by a dragon. Davidson carries on a heroic pursuit over the mountainous terrain, which as an outcast he has come to know well, and he reaches her retreat.

Though Diana naturally objects, Davidson seizes her celestial spear and kills her dragon, in the best Spenserian tradition, while Diana, in the best Victorian tradition, sighs over her dead dragon with, according to Davidson, "Such sad gesture, such abandonment/ Of deity forlorn, and so divine/ A tenderness that I forbore to look" (63). After he kills her dragon, he makes his *bēot* to her: "I am the foe of all the gods. I slew/ Apollo, Thor, Aidoneus" (62). Although he protests he does not like goddesses, he talks to her for a long time. Davidson is one of only four people who have had the power to see her, the virgin deity says. She wants him to tell her what mortals say about her encounters with Orion and Actaeon, but she does not wish to hear about Endymion. Davidson tells her anyway.

After relating the story of Endymion to her, she seems "about to fade and crumble" in his sight, and he vows "she should not perish thus" (72). Then he makes the mistake of partaking of some nectar and ambrosia which he gives to her: a materialist has no business partaking of the food of the gods. Nevertheless, the combination of his heroic materialism and the ambrosia and nectar gives him a "supremacy no spirit could withstand" (174), and he leads her into an arbor, overjoyed to think that he should "here deflower the undeflowered/ Immortal blossom of virginity" (75). Diana recalls in dismay that the prophet Proteus told her centuries ago that some man would overcome her.

Before the seduction takes place, another long conversation ensues when Diana demands to know how Davidson vanquished Aidoneus, Thor, and Apollo. So he explains to her that he defeated Aidoneus in battle outside the gates of hell and then tossed the gates into the sea. After the destruction of the god of hell, hell itself blossomed into sudden spring;; thus, symbolically, the ideas of hell and sin are destroyed. As for Thor, after a day-long wrestling match with him, material overcame spiritual; symbolically, the destruction of Thor represents the triumph of Mammon over all spiritual ideas, especially of God or the gods. Then Davidson relates proudly and at length (88–106) to Diana how he defeated Apollo: in a singing match, of course. Apollo sang a great song of gods and men, heaven and hell, love and hatred, even repeated the "spheral music Troy was builded with" (91). Davidson tells her he was nearly overcome by Apollo's great music; however,

> Roused from my reverie not a word I spoke,
> But clasped my hands behind me, having no lyre
> And mightily against Apollo's song . . .
>
> .................................................................
> I waged the Universe itself. . . .
>
> (95–96)

In short, Davidson sang—the song of the message of materialism! He sang of how from the ether came the atoms, then how the nebulae formed themselves into the universe, and how man came to be through the scale of being. Near the end of his song, he told of the material origins of the ideas of God and the gods. The song of matter had such a deleterious effect upon Apollo that his voice faded, he shrank, and his harp rusted. Davidson knocked him down, tore him to pieces, and wrung him like a rag until he "ceased to be" (106). In destroying Apollo, Davidson, like the

Man Forbid, succeeds in cutting away his spiritual roots in the culture and literatures of the past. Having overcome the poetry of Apollo with his song of matter, he has symbolically destroyed literary traditions and replaced them with his own poetry of the universe become self-conscious.

Having completed the story of the conquests of Aidoneus, Thor, and Apollo, Davidson has persuaded even Diana herself that she is the final vestige of spirituality around. In her virginity, she stands for the spirituality of the love relationship (cf. *Diabolus Amans*), perhaps even for the Christian emphasis on chastity and sexual purity (see 117), and, in a larger sense, she may even be taken to suggest Christian charity or the Christian ethic. Having overcome gods that stand for hell and sin and the idea of God, as well as the literatures of the past with their emphasis upon the spiritual world, Davidson must finally rid the world of this holdover of religious ethics, love, by seducing the goddess of virginity. But he made the error of taking the food and nectar of the gods; and, instead of deflowering her derisively, he now wishes to enjoy her love with her consent.

He even admits to her the possibility of a dwelling place of the gods (119), and he tells her that "not a gnome or filmy elf,/ Demon or angel, hero, deity" can ever die (121). Allowing herself to be swayed by Davidson's soothing talk, Diana yields; and they go forth into the harmony of an amoral universe, in company with the nun of "The Ballad of a Nun." After the night of love, Diana's spirituality fades; she becomes a mere aged goddess, an old hag bent on lewdness. The enjoyment of spiritual food now works its effects upon Davidson, too, so that he suddenly dies; and, as punishment for seducing the goddess, wakes up in hell, not the Christian hell, but a hitherto unknown hell, "the Hell of Deity" (134).

In imagery that suggests Dante or Milton, Davidson describes the punishments suffered by the gods, who are impaled upon hooks throughout the vault of hell. For example,

> Upon a skewer, that through their navels stuck,
> Vulcan and Mars, with Venus wedged between,
> Bellowed discordant frenzy as they hit
> And clawed each other.
>
> (137)

And then he sees Diana, his "divine companion of the night," renewed in youth and beauty, who,

> Impaled throughout her sumptuous deity—
> Beside Athene strung upon a stake!—
> Wriggled and yelled abominably hurt.
>
> (139)

But not only Diana suffers for the night of love. Davidson then witnesses himself being crucified. In a hellish confusion of his normal perceptions, he is crucified while he watches himself being crucified—while John Davidson in his own person watches the John Davidson of the poem being crucified. As he explains it, he is punished because

> I, as man, was guilty of the gods,
> Guilty of God; and in myself partook
> Uniquely of the nature of the gods,
> Having supped upon their food, and having loved
> A deity, and been by her belov'd.
>
> (139)

Davidson has assumed the role of savior; he has taken upon himself the errors of the world and died in order to bring redemption to mankind. The world's error is its wish to hold on to ideas of the numinous in nature; for the time being, Davidson partakes of spiritual nourishment, but it is only so that he can bring immateriality to its absolute end that he does it. The seduction of Diana, made possible by his having professed belief in spiritual things, is a symbolic emancipation of mankind from an ethic of love. Davidson dies on the cross so that man might be redeemed from Christianity and enjoy a rich existence in an amoral universe. He dies so that man may have life, and have it more abundantly—but entirely in this world, never in the next: "Four persons in the God-head—the Sire, the Son,/ The Holy Spirit, and the Evil One" (140), cries Davidson from the cross, and instantly hell disappears. His own version of the harrowing of hell is complete. Having placed himself, the Evil One, or Mammon, or Materialistic Man, on a level with the Triune God, there is an ultimate, absolute eradication of all traces of immaterial being: even the Hell of

Deity disappears. Davidson finds himself back on the mountain where his adventure began.

As the poem ends, he summarizes what he has accomplished, both in the allegorical action of *The Testament of John Davidson* and in his total writings of the eight years from 1901 to 1908:

> Thus in my night adventure and my death
> I purged the world of the last remnant left
> Of Other World, the hideous Hell of the Gods,
> Of virgin worship, and, in myself, of God—
> Pernicious slander of material truth
> So terribly avenged in the last Hell.
> And thus I made the world a fit abode
> For greatness and the men who yet may be.
>                                         (140)

He has also rid himself of the last remnant of God: Mammon has overcome Oswald.

He has by this time, however, no very high hopes for reforming the world, for making the ultimate revaluation. He has laid the foundation; he has left the world the message of matter, and that is his calling. Whether others take it up no longer matters: "And though I make the mystery known to men,/ It may be none here-after shall achieve/ The perfect purpose of eternity" (141). Nevertheless, Davidson has in *The Testament of John Davidson* symbolically, and to his satisfaction, destroyed the last remaining traces of spiritual ideas, both in himself and in the mind of man.

## VII  *Suicide: The Final Triumph of the Will to Live*

Davidson in a note published as preface to the posthumous *Fleet Street and Other Poems* [38] wrote: "The time has come to make an end. There are several motives. I find my pension is not enough; I have therefore still to turn aside and attempt things for which people will pay. My health also counts. Asthma and other annoyances I have tolerated for years; but I cannot put up with cancer." As we have just observed, an element of calm resignation is evident in *The Testament of John Davidson,* and in the Epilogue to the testament, "The Last Journey," Davidson clearly spells out not only his resignation but also his despair:

> My feet are heavy now, but on I go,
>   My head erect beneath the tragic years.
> The way is steep, but I would have it so;
>   And dusty, but I lay the dust with tears,
> Though none can see me weep: alone I climb
> The rugged path that leads me out of time—
>     Out of time and out of all,
>     Singing yet in sun and rain,
>     "Heel and toe from dawn to dusk,
>     Round the world and home again."
>                                              (146)

The imagery of a journey, juxtaposed with images of death, suggests that Davidson is more than simply lamenting the approach of old age and the loss of poetic power. He is writing of his own death in the near future; the poem is almost his obituary.

Even in the prologue to *The Testament of John Davidson*, in what he calls a "poem of the dawn of life," he emphasizes death. Should the lovers of "Honeymoon" ever find life too frustrating and unhappy, then, the husband explains, they will get into a boat, head out to sea, and "Sink with the setting sun,/ And shelter our love in death/ Since our beautiful day is done" (38).

Thus, the solution to despair lies in death, specifically in suicide; this solution is one which Davidson had frequently proposed. As early as 1886, the autobiographical heroes of *Smith* commit suicide rather than endure the frustration that rises from trying to overcome an unheeding world. In 1895, Ninian in the eclogue, "Lammas," explains that suicide has been a source of strength to him; he has known that at any time he could cut off his existence, either at a time of great pleasure or of great despair and, during the later years, suicide, and the despair leading toward suicide, are quite often referred to in Davidson's writing.

Furthermore the five Testaments and *The Theatrocrat* all mention the heroic suicide. For example, among the heroes in the empire builder's heaven are those who died by their own hand, "Refusing life because they failed to break/ The world's hard heart." [39] In *The Prime Minister*, one of the characters refers to suicide as the "final triumph of the will to live." [40] Davidson explains this paradoxical statement in the prose epilogue to *Holiday and Other Poems*: of Romeo's death speech, he writes that "you are in the presence of the final triumph of the will to live, which every sane suicide must be; despair—really the highest power and sublimation of hope—choosing death rather than resignation; the will to live, the pride of life that *cannot* renounce, the beautiful, the transcendent passion whereby the world survives, destroying itself rather than want its will." [41]

This idea is treated more fully in a short story, "The Realms of the Ultimate Pole," published in 1905. The narrator says that circumstances require him to visit the North Pole periodically. One day he gets to musing there about his material nature (he is a Davidsonian materialist), and he wanders off across the ice and snow. Suddenly a great crack in the ice causes him to be dumped into the icy water. He is rescued by the strange inhabitants of an iceberg which comes by; they are the Alandoths, splendid heroic specimens with blood the temperature of molten metal. As he floats along, the Alandoths strike up music, and they all resolutely march off the iceberg into the sea, where they, of course, drown. The narrator concludes that they must be inhabitants of some unknown Arctic realm, who, finding themselves cast adrift, nobly commit suicide: "Their sustenance being exhausted, and knowing no means whereby they might return to the only atmosphere and region at all tolerable to their extraordinary nature, they had, in the pride of life and perfect possession of all their powers, stepped joyfully to their ocean grave rather than be for one moment of their existence anything less than puissant and splendid Alandoths." [42] The Alandoths are heroic characters, who, when they can no longer exist in a world unsuited for them, choose to die nobly and in possession of all their faculties rather than let circumstances slowly wear them down.

In *The Testament of John Davidson,* the hero plans to commit suicide. Man is a supreme creature, he says, because he may die when he wishes: "No other living thing can choose to die" (47). Suicide, as he sees it, is a heroic act; it is the ultimate overcoming of fate. Any heroic character should be willing to return to the ether from whence he came. When a heroic vitalist sees that he can no longer resist fate, that he is no longer an Overman, he should perform voluntary euthanasia:

> Men are the Universe
> Aware at last, and must not live in fear,
> Slaves of the seasons, padded, bolstered up,

> Clystered and drenched and dieted and drugged;
> Or hateful victims of senility,
> Toothless and like an infant checked and schooled;
> Or in the dungeon of a sick room drained
> By some tabescent horror in their prime;
> But when the tide of life begins to turn,
>
> ............................................................................
>
> Stand out to sea and bend our withered sails
> Against the sunset, valiantly resolved
> To win the haven of eternal night.

(47–48)

Davidson is speaking about his own ideas, but what the Davidson of the poem does is not to be taken as an imitation of the actions of John Davidson, the English poet. The hero of the poem is thus a kind of persona, and the action of the poem is symbolic action. Therefore, although Davidson talks about suicide in the poem, this fact does not mean that he actually went to a mountain to take his life and changed his mind. Davidson obviously advocates suicide as a heroic way of dying, but the hero's attempt at suicide is only a symbolic action. There is still some small esthetic distance between the hero of the poem and the author.

But on March 23, 1909, the identification between the poet and his persona was completed. Davidson the man followed the advice of Davidson the poet, and he took his own life at a time when he evidently thought circumstances were about to get the upper hand. Illness and loss of poetic powers no doubt brought him to the point of despair, but in a man of Davidson's courage, despair might also have simply rallied him to greater endurance.

If we seek the explanation of his suicide in his works, just as we traced his development in them, this final act is the logical end of his special mixture of heroic vitalism and materialism. The man who wills to live loves life—but he wants life on his terms, not on those which circumstances allow him. Thus suicide, as he said many times, allowed him to cheat fate and to win a triumph over a hostile environment. By taking his own life, the heroic vitalist, John Davidson, merely hastened his return to the material ether out of which he was evolved:

> Who kills
> Himself subdues the conqueror of kings:
> Exempt from death is he who takes his life:
> My time has come.[43]

# CHAPTER 7

## *"Art for Man"*

> One who could rehearse
> Unheard-of things; whose thoughts were gray
> With travail, and whose reason scarce
> Escaped the onslaught of the universe:
>
> Yet one who waged an equal strife,
> And, unsubdued, beyond the sad
> Horizon of terrestrial life
> In noisome cloud and thunder clad,
> And death-cries of the past that bade
> Repent, above the galaxy
> Enthroned himself; and, sane or mad,
> Magnanimously claimed to be
> The soul and substance of eternity.
>
> —John Davidson describing himself
> in "Liverpool Street Station," 1909 [1]

A S stated in the introduction, the purpose of this study is to seek Davidson's development in his books, as he suggested we should do. In following two central themes through his published works—poetry, drama, prose—as well as his letters, we have traced the growth of Davidson's mind.

## I  *The Style Is the Man*

Davidson's dedication to the gospel of materialism and heroism is a prophet's devotion to his message. His writings are his sermons. Considering the tradition of Scotch Protestantism out of which he came, his evangelistic fervor is no surprise, nor is his dedication to art for the sake of ideas or his rejection of "art for art's sake." "Art for Art is a great saying," Davidson wrote in 1902, "and great things have been done in the spirit of it; but the greatest things have been done in the spirit of another saying. . . .

Art for man." [2] Both Davidson's successes and failures in style are summed up in this quotation; for when he succeeded, he did so because he produced "Art for Man," but when he failed, he did so because he paid so little attention to art.

Davidson tried his hand at a great many genres and forms. In drama he wrote tragedies and comedies, dramatic recitations and thesis plays. In fiction he wrote short stories and novels. In poetry he wrote lyrics, ballads, eclogues, odes, dramatic monologues, narratives, small epics, and verse essays. In nonfictional prose he wrote reviews, criticism, travel narratives, and philosophical discourses. In short, nearly every literary mode in the English tradition was at some time a part of his repertory.

As a general rule, Davidson's style is most successful when he is most ironic, or, to say it another way, when there is the greatest distance between writer and persona; it is least successful when the personae all become John Davidson. Having said that, I should logically conclude that drama, which ordinarily furnishes the greatest esthetic distance, should have been Davidson's best genre, but it was not. The early plays are too derivative and trite in plot, and the later plays are mere media for the message. Seldom does one stay with a Davidson play to see how it will end.

Like the later plays, the narratives or little epics, such as the Testaments, fail in part at least because the art becomes completely subjugated to the message. The message is a strange one indeed, but one might tolerate its strangeness if the message were not set forth with such battering-ram-like directness. The speakers, whether they be empire builders or prime ministers or John Davidson, all mount the soapbox and pound their message home in heavy, tortured, and humorless blank verse. Sometimes of course we accept that sort of blank verse, as in parts of *Paradise Lost*, but then it seems appropriate to the circumstances, and we occasionally find relief from it in other passages. Not so in Davidson; the message is unrelenting and unrelieved. Art is forgotten; the message is all.

On the other hand, Davidson's fiction is seldom dominated by a message. Though none of his fiction appears (or should, for that matter) on reading lists of nineteenth-century fiction, the fiction generally has the quality of irony and objectivity about it. It is open, airy, light, and not unreadable, but at the same time, one would not take precious leisure time to read it as he might other minor nineteenth-century fiction. The plots are weak, and the stories at best pleasant, though usually ephemeral. Only *Earl Lavender* has about it something of the richness and applicability that we associate with the fiction we bother to remember, but even that novel is limited by its topicality and by a hodgepodge plot that is only barely held together by the person of Earl Lavender himself.

In the poems of the 1890's, especially the ballads and the eclogues, Davidson's character found its most artful expression. The style was the man in those poems: in the eclogues because they allowed him to be ironic and searching, and in the ballads because they allowed him to be straightforward and manly. We have seen again and again how these sides of his personality sought to be expressed. The eclogues were particularly successful in expressing Davidson's ironic searching, or, as he put it, his being a trembling lyre for every wind to sound. Davidson re-created the neo-classical eclogue, often placing it ironically in the city (as in *Fleet Street Eclogues,* for example), and used as speakers men of the publishing and journalistic world in which he earned his living, men who like him were caught in the crosscurrents of materialism, evolutionism, Social Darwinism, Nietzscheism, and imperialism. Though Davidson's eclogues are scarcely bucolic in tone, the generally low-keyed voices of the conversing shepherd-journalists of the eclogue allowed Davidson to explore the important existential questions of his day without undue commitment to any side and with a happy absence of the revivalistic sermonizing which always seemed to be pressing its way to the fore in his work.

The ballad form also served Davidson well, but for somewhat different reasons. He was able to sustain the short narrative sequences of the ballads in a way which he could not do in longer narratives, whether fiction or the narratives of the Testaments. Thus the stories of the "Ballad of a Nun" or the "Ballad of Heaven," for example, are carried through with a refreshing clarity and directness, without any sacrificing of the theme or the "Art for Man" that Davidson believed in. Also the ballad provided a medium that was traditionally bold and resolute, giving the masculine directness of Davidson a voice; and yet the ballad is also traditionally objective, with the narrator submerged in the story, thus keeping Davidson from overinvolving himself in the poem. In short, Davidson's style was best in his short poems when the form he chose merged his ironic questioning, or the scientific side of the man, with his Evangelical sturdiness, or the Scottish Protestant side.

## II  Davidson's Ideas: A Concluding Estimate

As a reformer and poet of ideas, Davidson was fully in the tradition of nineteenth-century English thought, though Continental writings helped form his ideas. Blake, one of the early English Romantic reformers and system builders, was strongly influential in the marriage of good and evil which Davidson effected during the 1890's. Burns, another Scot and another poet of protest, surely inspired some of Davidson's iconoclasm. Carlyle undoubtedly provided a major impetus in Davidson's early protests against creedal Christianity and also in his early commitment to supernatural naturalism. Davidson also learned from Carlyle to worship the man who sees his duty and does it, and he may also have developed his latter-day veneration of empire building from Carlyle's "might means right," with an assist from John Adam Cramb. Browning, too, showed Davidson that life is a battle and that man's business is to carry on one fight more against fate. From Nietzsche, Davidson later gathered authority for ideas already developed in his own early works. His Davidsonian hero paralleled Nietzsche's Overman; his dislike of unheroic ennui and remorse paralleled Nietzsche's hatred of the Christian "slave morality," and, from his study of Nietzsche, his ideas gained new clarity and force.

Meanwhile, the scientists Darwin, Spencer, and Huxley had impressed the predisposed Davidson with the reasonableness of their empiric investigations into the nature of man and the universe, and by 1901 he was prepared to render up scientific materialism as a new poetry. Out of the ashes of the orthodoxy which he destroyed rose the phoenix of a new religion of materialism and heroism which brought together the two great subjects of Victorian literature, science and religion. Ideas of Blake, Burns, Carlyle, Browning, and Nietzsche merged with those of Darwin, Huxley, and Spencer to produce a distinctly Davidsonian religion with man as God and himself as one of the Godhead.

Thus in Davidson's writings much of nineteenth-century thought culminates. All the familiar strains of English Romantic and Victorian literature are present. The final plays and testaments point an ominous finger into the twentieth century. Davidson's superman-hero Mammon is uncomfortably like some modern reformers who have in the name of freedom only forged more manacles.

The question we must inevitably face is whether or not Davidson's ideas are after all worth anything. He was not the only writer to try to solve the science-religion conflict and to work out his salvation in the process. He was not the only one to ask questions and to seek honest answers. The superman reformer would have come to be without Davidson's imaginative portrait. He influenced few people, if any.[3] As A. E. Housman said to Grant Richards about Davidson: "As for his knowledge which is going to change the world, it is just like the doctrine of the Trinity: probably false, and quite unimportant if true." [4] The materialistic theory does not seem to make much difference, perhaps because it offers no better solutions to man's problems than the traditional answers. As A. S. Mories wrote of Davidson, "New Gods can only vindicate their claim by coming home to the human spirit and answering its deepest needs in a way that the older Gods are failing to do. This is where Davidson's Herculean crusade fails." [5]

Furthermore, those plays and poems where we see Davidson's hero changing the world present to our hindsight no pleasant prospect. In short, Davidson's ideas have proved wrong: Christianity has turned out not to be the "dead corpse" that he said it was; and hero worship has failed as a solution to our problems. Empire building and racial chauvinism are anachronisms as ugly as Mammon's thumbscrew and rack. Our world, precariously balanced between cold war and annihilation, cannot afford to turn loose a hero bent on self-expression, depending absolutely on his infallible intuition.

But ideas come and go; one age's ideology is often the next age's anathema. And many a writer whom we may still read with pleasure works within a now outdated system of thought. The fact that Davidson's ideas are no longer fashionable does not mean we must discredit him. Indeed, even considering the jingoistic and chauvinistic and materialistic excesses of the later years, there is much to admire in Davidson. As I have said, religion and science are his great subjects, and as every man must do who thinks at all, he attempts to work out his salvation with fear and trembling. Finding the conventional means of salvation not to his liking, he went on to create his own. And in the very noblest Victorian tradition—Carlyle, Tennyson, Browning, Arnold, Hopkins, Hardy are his peers—he makes a courageous effort to resolve the great dilemma between science and religion.

In his productive period, from 1893 (*Fleet Street Eclogues*) to 1908, who in English literature surpasses him in the sincerity and boldness and artistry of his search for salvation? There are few who do; and those few do it, not because they deal with greater themes, but because they have something more than Davidson in the way of artistic discipline. Of the members of the Rhymers' Club, only W. B. Yeats achieved more than Davidson: Ernest Dowson, Lionel Johnson, and Arthur Symons are but historic examples of "Art for Art." Kipling and Henley are better known names than Davidson, but probably no more often read. Thomas Hardy had just resumed his career as a poet, and George Meredith's career was pretty much over by 1893. In the drama Shaw still lives by virtue of the wit of his plays, not because his ideas are necessarily superior to Davidson's.

Thus, Davidson's worth as a writer is enhanced a good deal when he is compared with his contemporaries. Only a few major writers—Yeats, Hardy, Shaw—tower over him. In an age of decadence, an age of minor writers and minor poetry, Davidson tried very hard to be not a minor poet but a major prophet. Even his failures are compelling. The Testaments and the Mammon plays, for example, demand the reader's attention, yet none can be called artistically satisfying. They fail because Davidson lets ideas dominate the action absolutely; though the Testaments are dramatic monologues, they do not objectify Davidson's ideas: they merely recite them. Though he creates characters in the Mammon plays, the characters are his puppets and spokesmen, whose very word and deed are dictated by the demands of the author's message.

Thus, Davidson was only partly successful, but paradoxically, what success he attained, he attained because of his ideas. "A Ballad in Blank Verse of the Making or a Poet," "A Ballad of Heaven," "A Ballad of Hell," "A Ballad of a Nun," and "A Runnable Stag," the eclogues "Lammas" and "St. George's Day," *The Testament of a Man Forbid* and *The Testament of John Davidson,* the chronicle play *Bruce*, the novel *Earl Lavender*—these are memorable because they are "art for man," because of, not in spite of, Davidson's ideas. In the 1890's and in the early 1900's Davidson's concern with the great Victorian and eminently modern theme of religion marks him as a distinctly strong masculine voice among a chorus of lesser, and, may I say, effeminate voices.

Not only the ideas, but the forceful presentation of the ideas compels one to remember Davidson. He was never willing to grant that beauty counts more than ideas, or power; and, though this neglect of technique may have been his weakness, his concern with ideas and their fervent expression is his strength. Davidson is a poet whom one cannot read without remembering: after all, one remembers a man who has such refreshingly great ambition as to wish to be a trembling lyre for every wind to sound, to be prince of the powers of the air, and lord of the world; and who, finding the world unsatisfactory, would have it on no terms but his own. The small man says, "I am unfit for this world"; the great man says, "This world is unfit for me." The small man concludes that he must either destroy himself or adjust to this world; the great man says, "I will destroy this unfit world and make it over again in my own image." [6] There is something unforgettable about a man like that, and John Davidson was such a man.

## III  *A Postscript on Davidson's Materialism*

I said in the preface that a study of Davidson provides a way of understanding our current value crisis. It seems that Davidson's work in some way illustrates nearly every set of values that is competing for our commitment in the last third of the twentieth century: humane, religious, material, imperialistic, and Fascistic. As he said, he was a trembling lyre for every wind to sound.

Material, imperialistic, and Fascistic value orientations have had their day since Davidson wrote of them, and we have seen the disastrous results. Yet the systems created by these values die hard, and, in fact, seem to be alive and well—especially materialism and Fascism—in spite of ample illustrations of their destruction of the human spirit. Davidson's career seems to be a prototype of the outcome of commitment to these values. The humane and religious values demonstrated as early as *Diabolus Amans* (1885) and underlying "Thirty Bob a Week" (1894) were overwhelmed by materialism and worship of force, so that by 1900 the only Davidson voices to be heard were those of strident materialism and shrill hero worship. Simultaneously, Davidson's "Art for Man," as he called it, declined, so that the materialistic and heroic writings are to us at very best objects of historical inquiry, compelling by their ambition and eagerness but ultimately esthetically and morally repugnant. At the same time, Davidson's alienation from his fellow man increased, so that finally he was the "Man Forbid," cut off from his human roots, and the result was, as we have seen, more and more bizarre and inhumane utterances and, eventually, suicide.

In short, materialism and worship of power long ago proved to be destructive of man, indeed the very man who gave himself to those value systems. But the Davidson that has survived also illustrates value systems: the humane, the tolerant, the ironic, the questioning Davidson is still readable. In his career, those deeply human values once more have demonstrated their long-term worth; the quiet voice of Davidson is still speaking, but the strident voice is stilled. The meek may not have yet inherited the earth, but Davidson's career reminds us that meekness has remarkable staying power.

# Notes and References

## Chapter One

1. London *Times*, April 19, 1909, p. 10. See James Benjamin Townsend, *John Davidson: Poet of Armageddon* (New Haven, 1961), pp. 1–28, for a full discussion of the events surrounding Davidson's suicide.

2. R. M. Wenley, "Introduction" to *Poems by John Davidson* (New York, 1924), p. viii.

3. Wenley, p. x.

4. In collaboration with C. J. Wills, *Laura Ruthven's Widowhood* (London, 1892), Vol. 2, p. 36.

5. Harold Williams, *Modern English Writers* (New York, 1919), p. 25.

6. Townsend, p. 29.

7. Douglas Bush, *Mythology and the Romantic Tradition* (Cambridge, 1937), p. 468.

8. Letter dated April 27, 1897, from the Grosvenor Club, New Bond St[.], London W[.]; quoted in Townsend, pp. 472–73; my italics.

## Chapter Two

1. *Diabolus Amans* (Glasgow, 1885); *The North Wall* (Glasgow, 1885); *Bruce* (Glasgow, 1886); *Smith* (Glasgow, 1888); *Plays* (Greenock, 1889).

2. Townsend, pp. 58–59. *In a Music-Hall* was published in London by Ward and Downey.

3. We must accept Davidson's dates for the composition of the plays, but there is no particular reason to doubt his honesty about them. See *Scaramouch in Naxos and other Plays* (London, 1890), p. 5, for the date of this play. Davidson says the poems in the volume *In a Music-Hall and other Poems* (London, 1891), other than the title poem, were written between 1872 and 1889 but "are not arranged in the order of composition" (15). There is no way of assigning dates to these poems, so we must take *An Unhistorical Pastoral* as the earliest datable work.

4. See *Scaramouch in Naxos*, p. 87 and *Plays* (London, 1894), p. 83. References in my text are to the page numbers of *Plays*, 1894.

## Notes and References

5. Quoted in Townsend, pp. 48–49. See also the high praise of Browning in the untitled leader on Robert Browning in *The Glasgow Herald* (December 14, 1889), 6, on the occasion of Browning's death.

6. Written 1884, first published in Glasgow in 1886. See *Plays*, 1894, p. 125, for the date of composition. References in my text are to page numbers in the collected *Plays*, 1894.

7. References in my text are to page numbers in the 1885 edition, the only edition of the poem.

8. Cf. Paul Tillich: "Therefore, let us keep open our ears and let us keep open our hearts, and ask with great seriousness and great passion: Is there a word from the Lord, a word for me, here and now, a word for our world in this moment? It *is* there, it tries to come to you. Keep open for it!" *The New Being* (New York, 1955), p. 124.

9. What "offends the taste and shocks the sense" of the poet is the "pagan sacrifice" of the "body and the blood" as celebrated in the communion service.

10. In the short poem, "On a Hill-top," Davidson describes a mystical experience, *In A Music-Hall*, pp. 88–90.

11. Carlton J. H. Hayes, *A Generation of Materialism: 1871–1900* (New York, 1941), pp. 138–40.

12. Clearly Davidson knows wrong from right, sin from virtue; it is incorrect to say, as Townsend does, that at this point "moral and spiritual choice are waived altogether or become wholly empirical; sin and virtue are synonymous" (Townsend, 115). This may describe Davidson's morality in later years, but not at the time this poem was written.

13. *The North Wall* (Glasgow, 1885). References in my text are to page numbers in the first edition. The novel was later reprinted as *The Practical Novelist* in *The Great Men and a Practical Novelist* (London, 1891).

14. I am indebted to the chapter on Romantic Irony in Irving Babbitt, *Rousseau and Romanticism* (Boston, 1919), for these ideas about the irony of the questioning Romantic.

15. Self-parody must surely be related to the sort of parading of perversity which we associate with the last Romantics, such as Oscar Wilde's *Dorian Gray*, for example.

16. *In a Music-Hall*, pp. 21–24.

17. *Ibid.*, pp. 31–35.

18. See the collected *Plays* (1894), p. 217, for the date of composition. Published as *Smith: a Tragedy* (Glasgow, 1888), republished in *Plays* (London, 1894), and "now called, as originally intended, 'A Tragic Farce,'" p. [v]. References in my text are to the page numbers in *Plays*, 1894. I wish to correct two factual errors in Townsend's description of the play. He says: "*Smith*, written in 1885, the year in

which *Diabolus Amans* appeared . . ." (124); the correct date is 1886. Townsend has the correct date on p. 340 n. He also says, "It is chiefly in blank verse with interspersed songs" (124). However, the play is entirely in blank verse except for one eight-syllable line (1. 6, p. 224); there are no songs.

19. See *Smith*, pp. 223 and 226. These details agree in general with Davidson's career up to 1886—teaching from 1877 to 1884, clerking in a Glasgow thread firm in 1884 and 1885.

20. *North Wall*, pp. 97–98.

21. *Diabolus Amans*, p. 38. This theme of perfect love ending in death is treated in two poems from *In a Music-Hall*, "For Lovers," see especially p. 71, and "Anselm and Bianca," pp. 36–44.

22. There is possibly some influence here of Schopenhauer on Davidson's thought. See, for example, this passage from Schopenhauer: "Far from being denial of the will, suicide is a phenomenon of strong assertion of will; for the essence of negation lies in this, that the joys of life are shunned, not its sorrows. The suicide wills life, and is only dissatisfied with the conditions under which it has presented itself to him. He therefore by no means surrenders the will to live, but only life, in that he destroys the individual manifestation." Arthur Schopenhauer, *The World as Will and Idea*, trans. R. B. Haldane and J. Kemp, 3rd ed. (London, 1891), 3 vols., vol. 1, pp. 514–15. To some extent, this passage explains how Davidson's characters can affirm life, yet seek death through suicide. However, Schopenhauer does not recommend suicide, as Davidson does.

23. Published in *Plays* (Greenock, 1889), which was reissued as *Scaramouch in Naxos: a Pantomime and other Plays* (London, 1890). References in my text are to the latter edition. See p. 129 for the date of composition.

### Chapter Three

1. See Townsend, pp. 175–78, for an account of some of the parodies.

2. *Ballads and Songs* (London, 1894), pp. 7–35; references in my text are to page numbers in this edition.

3. Friedrich Nietzsche, *Thus Spake Zarathustra*, trans. Alexander Tille, rev. M. M. Bozman (London, 1933), pp. 253–60.

4. See John A. Lester, Jr., "Friedrich Nietzsche and John Davidson: a Study in Influence," *Journal of the History of Ideas*, XVIII (June, 1957), 411–29, for the best discussion of the Nietzsche-Davidson relationship. Lester has treated the problem about as conclusively as it can be treated in our present state of knowledge about Davidson. See also Gertrude von Petzold, *John Davidson, und Sein Geistiges Werden unter*

*dem Einfluss Nietzsche* (Leipzig, 1928). Her conclusions about the early influence of Nietzsche on Davidson are largely undercut because she assumed that the reference to Nietzsche in Davidson's *Sentences and Paragraphs* (1893) is evidence of his firsthand knowledge of Nietzsche's published German works. She does not take into account (1) Davidson's admission that he did not read German, nor (2) the fact that Davidson's early knowledge of Nietzsche came secondhand from the very summary French article by de Wyzewa. Two volumes of Nietzsche appeared early in French translation, *Richard Wagner à Bayreuth* (1877), and *Le Cas Wagner* (1893), but even had he read them, neither of these works would have been much of an influence on Davidson's thought.

5. Lester, p. 417.

6. Note that Davidson spells Nietzsche like de Wyzewa did—Nietsche—indicating that he probably had not seen the name in German. His *Glasgow Herald* article concludes with this statement: "Any man who has work to do in the world, any man who has children, any man who enjoys ordinary health is furnished with an answer to Nietsche."

7. Oscar Levy, "The Nietzsche Movement in England," in *Complete Works of Nietzsche*, ed. Oscar Levy, 18 vols. (London, 1909, 1914–1924), vol. 18, p. ix. Lester lists other early references to Nietzsche in English, p. 417 n. The translations were *The Case of Wagner, Nietzsche contra Wagner, The Twilight of the Idols*, and *The Anti-Christ*, trans. Thomas Common, published in one volume (London, 1896); *Thus Spake Zarathustra*, trans. Alexander Tille (London, 1896); and *Genealogy of Morals* and *Poems*, trans. W. A. Haussman and John Gray, in one volume (London, 1897).

8. See Jane T. Stoddard, "An Interview with Mr. John Davidson," *Bookman*, I (March, 1895), p. 86.

9. *A Rosary* (London, 1903), pp. 188–90.

10. *A Random Itinerary* (London, 1894); references in my text are to page numbers in this edition.

11. *New Ballads* (London, 1897), p. 45. Ninian in the eclogue "Lammas," *A Second Series of Fleet Street Eclogues* (London, 1895), p. 127, speaks for Davidson when he says,

> Sometimes when I forget myself I talk
> As though I were persuaded of the truth
> Of some received or unreceived belief;
> But always afterwards I am ashamed
> Of such lewd lapses into bigotry.

In the same poem, Ninian does talk as though he were persuaded of the truth of the idea of heroism.

12. *Earl Lavender* (London, 1895). Page numbers cited in my text refer to this edition. Davidson defends *Earl Lavender* in a letter to the editor of the *Pall Mall Gazette* (February 21, 1895), p. 3. He says, "My purpose was sincere laughter, good-natured irony." In the remainder of the article Davidson acknowledges literary influences, a thing he was not wont to do. See *Time Magazine* (May 27, 1966) for an article about Beardsley and a reproduction of the frontispiece from *Earl Lavender*.

13. R. M. Metz, *A Hundred Years of British Philosophy* (London and New York, 1938), p. 108.

14. Dated from St. Winifred's, Fairmile Avenue, Streatham, S.W., October 29, 1898; original in British Museum (Ashley M.S. B. 572). Quoted in Townsend, pp. 467–68. The italics in the phrase, "must accept no creed," are mine.

15. *Earl Lavender*, p. 282.

16. "Thirty Bob a Week," first published in *The Yellow Book* (July, 1894), pp. 99–102; reprinted in *Ballads and Songs*, pp. 91–97. Page numbers in my text refer to this edition. See T. S. Eliot, Preface to *John Davidson: A Selection of his Poems*, ed. Maurice Lindsay (London, 1961), pp. xi–xii.

17. "Tête-à-Tête. John Smith, John Davidson," *Daily Chronicle* (November 14, 1898), p. 3.

18. "The Art of Poetry," *Speaker* (February 4, 1899), p. 154.

19. "Tête-à-Tête. Lord Brumm, Earl Lavender," *Speaker* (August 12, 1899), p. 154.

20. *Ballads and Songs*, p. 35.

21. *Miss Armstrong's and other Circumstances* (London, 1896), pp. 1–29. Page numbers in my text refer to this edition. In a bibliographic note Davidson explains that the story had appeared earlier: "The first portion of it appeared in the last number of the *Weekly Review*, a gallant, short-lived periodical, which I subedited in 1890; and the latter half was published as a complete story in the *Hawk*" (p. [v]). See "Miss Rollingstone's Failure," *Hawk* (April 28, 1891), pp. 467–68. Thus the story represents Davidson's ideas about art in 1890 as well as 1896, the year of publication in book form.

22. "Tête-à-Tête. John Smith, John Davidson," *Speaker* (March 11, 1899), p. 289. The speaker in the passage quoted is Davidson, not Smith.

23. *Ibid.*

24. *Fleet Street Eclogues* (London, 1893), pp. 15–27. Page numbers in my text refer to this edition.

25. "Poetry and the Something Behind Phenomena," *Speaker* (March 25, 1899), p. 346.

26. "Irony," *Speaker* (April 22, 1899), p. 455.

27. "Irony," *Speaker* (May 6, 1899), p. 323.

28. "Ballad of a Nun," first published in the *Yellow Book* (October, 1894), pp. 273–79; reprinted in *Ballads and Songs*, pp. 52–61, from which I quote. Townsend has traced thoroughly the minor sensation the poem created among the London literati; there are at least two parodies of it. See Townsend, pp. 173–78.

29. Cf. Blake, who held wild theories about sexual freedom, yet apparently had an ideally happy and respectable marriage. See David Erdmann, *Blake: Prophet Against Empire* (Princeton, 1954), p. 355.

30. Dated from 20 Park Riding, Hornsey N., November 29, 1894; original in Princeton University Library. The italics are mine. Davidson often expresses his liking for strong women. For example, in a review of Strindberg's *The Father*, Davidson writes: "I like Laura, the strong, healthy, middle-class woman. I have seen her shopping by the hundred in Holloway Road, in Regent Street, in Brixton, in Westbourne Grove; nice, blond creatures, with steady eyes and resolute utterance, their minds entirely occupied with dress and food, and their families and friends. Laura is admirable. . . ." "Tête-à-Tête. Lord Brumm, Earl Lavender," *Speaker* (August 12, 1899), pp. 153–54.

31. *New Ballads*, p. 117. The poem first appeared in *Saturday Review* (June 27, 1896), pp. 642–44; edited and reprinted in *New Ballads*, pp. 100–114. Page numbers in my text refer to this edition.

32. Townsend, p. 115.

33. *A Rosary*, p. 20.

34. Walter Kaufmann, *Nietzsche: Philosopher, Psychologist, Antichrist* (Princeton, 1950), p. 94.

35. "On the Downs," *Speaker* (February 5, 1898), p. 179; excerpts are reprinted in *A Rosary*, pp. 25–28.

36. Lester, pp. 419–20.

37. *Baptist Lake*, p. 66.

38. Lester, p. 422.

39. "Eclogue on the Downs," *Anglo-Saxon Review* (June, 1900), pp. 196–204; edited and reprinted in *A Rosary*, pp. 143–57. Page numbers in my text refer to *A Rosary*.

40. *Thus Spake Zarathustra*, translation and introduction by R. J. Hollingdale (Baltimore: Penguin Books, 1961), p. 61.

41. *Ballads and Songs*, pp. 62–71. Page numbers in my text refer to this edition.

## Chapter Four

1. These lines from *Beowulf* are a good example of an ancient heroic defiance of fate: "Wyrd oft nereð/ Unfaegne eorl, þonne his ellen dēah!"

2. See Jerome Hamilton Buckley, *William Ernest Henley: A Study in the "Counter-Decadence" of the Nineties* (Princeton, 1945).

3. *The Case of Wagner; Nietzsche contra Wagner; The Twilight of the Idols; The Anti-Christ*, 1896. *Thus Spake Zarathustra*, 1896. *A Genealogy of Morals; Poems*, 1897.

4. Eric Bentley, *A Century of Hero-Worship* (Philadelphia and New York, 1944), p. 257.

5. *Perfervid: The Career of Ninian Jamieson* (London, 1890). Page references in my text are to this edition.

6. "The Salvation of Nature," first published in *The Great Men* and *A Practical Novelist* (London, 1891); reprinted in *Pilgrimage of Strongsoul* (London, 1896), pp. 245–78; page references in my text are to this edition. Another story on the same theme is "Among the Anarchists" in *Miss Armstrong's and other Circumstances*, pp. 189–201.

7. *Ballads and Songs*, p. 97.

8. *Ibid.*, pp. 84–85.

9. "A Study of Ben Jonson," *Academy* (November 23, 1889), p. 331.

10. "Books in the Open Air," *Star* (March 10, 1898), p. 1.

11. *Prophetic Writings*, ed. Sloss and Wallis, vol. 1, p. 18.

12. *Laura Ruthven's Widowhood*, vol. 3, pp. 218–19.

13. *A Second Series of Fleet Street Eclogues* (London, 1895), pp. 11–43. Page references in my text are to this edition.

14. Townsend, p. 163.

15. "Tête-à-Tête. Lord Brumm, Earl Lavender," *Speaker* (August 12, 1899), p. 154. In 1893 Davidson had written that "nothing will persuade me that the whole race of men is not benefited physically and mentally by the preservation of the feeblest human life, that the fittest will survive in growing proporition as the unfit are tended." "A Suburban Philosopher," *Glasgow Herald* (April 22, 1893), p. 9.

16. Lester, p. 421.

17. *Ibid.*, pp. 423–24.

18. "The Aristocrat," *Last Ballad* (London, 1899), pp. 149–50; first published as "The Aristocrat: New Style," *Saturday Review* (August 20, 1898), p. 232.

19. *A Second Series of Fleet Street Eclogues*, pp. 75–101. Page references in my text are to this edition.

20. *Godfrida* (London, 1898); *Self's the Man* (London, 1901), written in 1899, according to p. ii; *Knight of the Maypole* (London, 1903), written 1900, see p. iv.

21. Pp. 68–69; see also "Prologue," p. 4.

22. P. 122. The speech is remarkably like Smith's in *Smith*; see *Plays*, p. 230: "But you are right: one must become/ Fanatic—be a wedge—a thunderbolt,/ To smite a passage through the close-grained world."

23. *Self's the Man* (London, 1901). Page references in my text are to this edition.

24. *Speaker* (March 15, 1898), pp. 297–98.

25. "Lammas" in *A Second Series of Fleet Street Eclogues,* p. 19. The speaker is Ninian (Ninny?).

26. R. M. Wenley, Introduction to *Poems by John Davidson,* p. viii.

27. Wenley, p. ix.

28. Wenley, p. xii.

### Chapter Five

1. "Hors-D'Oeuvre," *Westminster Gazette* (March 6, 1903), 2; reprinted in *A Rosary,* p. 19.

2. *A Rosary,* p. 86; reprinted from "Caviare," *Pall Mall Gazette* (May 30, 1903), 2.

3. James Douglas, quoted in the advertisements in *The Testament of a Man Forbid* (London, 1901), p. 2.

4. London *Times* (April 19, 1909), p. 10.

5. Note Nietzsche's emphasis on pain. See Walter Kaufmann, *Nietzsche,* pp. 238–40.

6. *Ballads and Songs,* pp. 69–70.

7. *The Testament of an Empire Builder* (London, 1902). Page references in my text are to this edition. *The Testament of a Man Forbid* will be discussed at the end of this chapter.

8. Townsend, pp. 343–44.

9. *The Testament of a Prime Minister* (London, 1904). Page references in my text are to this edition.

10. Townsend, p. 349.

11. *The Theatrocrat* (London, 1905), pp. 41–42.

12. "In my ballads I have employed this myth of God and Sin and Heaven and Hell as the warp of myth in the loom of my poetry, giving the myth also a new orientation as the weaver changes the pattern of his web—an orientation which I have carried to its utmost limit in the Judgment-day of the 'Prime Minister'...." *The Theatrocrat,* pp. 32–33.

13. Metz, p. 113.

14. William Irvine, *Apes, Angels, and Victorians* (New York, 1955), p. 136.

15. Townsend, p. 337.

16. "Alembroth," *The Academy* (May 14, 1904), 548.

17. *The Theatrocrat: A Tragic Play of Church and Stage* (London, 1905). Page references in my text are to this edition.

18. "Wordsworth's Immorality and Mine.—II," *The Outlook* (June 17, 1905), 873.

19. "On Poetry," *Holiday and Other Poems* (London, 1906), p. 137.

20. *Ibid.*, p. 138.

21. *Ibid.*, pp. 139–40.

22. *Ibid.*, p. 142.

23. *The Theatrocrat*, p. 27.

24. *Ibid.*, p. 57.

25. *The Testament of a Prime Minister*, p. 67. Subsequent page references in my text are to the 1904 edition.

26. *Diabolus Amans*, p. 75.

27. *Theatrocrat*, p. 77.

28. *Ibid.*, p. 32.

29. "The Theatrocrat," *Westminster Gazette* (December 11, 1905), 4.

30. Letter to William Archer, dated October 22, 1904, from 9 Fairmile Avenue, Streatham, S.W., original in British Museum, quoted in Townsend, p. 361.

31. *Theatrocrat*, p. 17, gives 1904 as the date of composition, though the play was published in 1905.

32. *Ibid.*, p. 26.

33. *The Testament of a Man Forbid* (London, 1901). Page references in my text are to this edition.

34. Townsend says, "Evidently by 1904 he was in such desperate need of money that he conquered all scruples, for in that year Lane published under Davidson's supervision a volume of his lyrics, *Selected Poems*. In deference to the wishes of the poet, the volume contained as its last selection the entire text of *The Testament of a Man Forbid*" (p. 357).

35. "Here Awa', There Awa'," *Outlook* (May 13, 1905), 680.

36. *The Theatrocrat*, written in 1904 (London, 1905). Page references in my text are to this edition.

37. For an account of the unfavorable reception of the play, see Townsend, pp. 364–75.

38. See "Wordsworth's Immorality and Mine, IV," *Outlook* (July 22, 1905), 95–96, for Davidson's comments on the meaning of the title.

39. "Epilogue," *Triumph of Mammon* (London, 1907), p. 165.

40. "Theatrocratic: Mr. John Davidson and his Surprising New Play," *Daily Chronicle* (November 28, 1905), 3.

41. The poem, "A Runnable Stag" was first published in the *Pall Mall Magazine* (July–December, 1905), 231–33, under the title, "A Ballad of a Runnable Stag." Retitled and reprinted in *Holiday and Other Poems*, pp. 14–19. Page references in my text are to this edition. The form and the alliterative element in this poem reflect Davidson's imitation of Poe; see *Holiday and Other Poems*, pp. 154–55.

### Chapter Six

1. *The Testament of an Empire Builder* (London, 1902). Page references in my text are to this edition.

2. "Ode on the Coronation of Edward VII., of Britain and of Greater Britain, King," *The Daily Chronicle* (August 9, 1902), 5, from which I quote in my text; edited and reprinted in *A Rosary*, pp. 6–11. Page references in my text are to *A Rosary*.

3. John Adam Cramb, *The Origin and Destiny of Imperial Britain* (London, 1900).

4. Townsend, p. 485.

5. Letter to Edmund Gosse, dated December 24, 1900; quoted in Townsend, p. 485.

6. "The Twenty-Fourth of May," *Holiday and Other Poems*, pp. 67–76; first published in *Outlook* (May 20, 1905), 721.

7. "Caviare," *Pall Mall Gazette* (May 30, 1903), 1.

8. "Blank Verse," *Outlook* (April 29, 1905), 613–14.

9. *A Rosary*, p. 6.

10. *Holiday and Other Poems*, p. 149.

11. "Alembroth," *The Academy* (May 14, 1904), 548.

12. *The Theatrocrat*, p. 58.

13. *The Testament of an Empire-Builder*, pp. 76–77.

14. *The Testament of a Prime Minister* (London, 1904). Page references in my text are to this edition.

15. See the poem, "The Testament of Sir Simon Simplex Concerning Automobilism," *Fleet Street and Other Poems* (London, 1909), pp. 100–110, which is a poetic protest against democracy.

16. "The Triumph of Mammon," *Times Literary Supplement* (May 3, 1907), 143.

17. "From Totnes to Penzance," *Glasgow Herald* (May 25, 1907), 11.

18. *Mammon and His Message* (London, 1908), pp. 149–50.

19. John A. Lester, Jr., "Friedrich Nietzsche and John Davidson: A Study in Influence," *Journal of the History of Ideas*, XVIII (1957), 424.

20. "The Theatrocrat," *Westminster Gazette* (December 11, 1905), 4.

21. "Theatrocratic: Mr. John Davidson and his Surprising New Play," *Daily Chronicle* (November 28, 1905), 3.

22. Benjamin Ifor Evans, *English Poetry in the Later Nineteenth Century* (London, 1933), pp. 288–89.

23. "At the Judgment-Seat: Mr. John Davidson Replies to his Critics," *Daily Chronicle* (December 20, 1905), 3.

24. *The Triumph of Mammon* (London, 1907), pp. 151–52.

25. *The Triumph of Mammon* (London, 1907). Page references in my text are to this edition. See Townsend, p. 389, for the details of the publication of this play.

26. See the scene description, p. 5, for example, or pp. 63–78 and 79.

27. *Mammon and His Message* (London, 1908). Page references in my text are to this edition.

28. See pp. 130–34 and 139.

29. "Lammas," *A Second Series of Fleet Street Eclogues*, p. 36.

30. "Lammas," p. 37.

31. To illustrate how far Davidson's ideas in 1908 are from those of his early and middle periods, we might compare what he has to say in 1893 on the subject of the preservation of the weak: "Nothing will persuade me that the whole race of man is not benefited physically and mentally by the preservation of the feeblest human life, that the fittest will survive in growing proportion as the unfit are tended." "A Suburban Philosopher," *Glasgow Herald* (April 22, 1893), 9.

32. *The Theatrocrat*, pp. 46–47. See also "The Isthmus at the Land's End," *Glasgow Herald* (December 7, 1907), 9; "Through the Sieve," *Westminster Gazette* (August 22, 1908), 14, for similar ideas.

33. "The Testament of a Juryman," *Westminster Gazette* (January 21, 1905), 2.

34. Townsend, pp. 402–3.

35. *Mammon and His Message*, pp. 169–73.

36. *The Testament of John Davidson* (London, 1908), from which I quote in my text.

37. Townsend, p. 414.

38. *Fleet Street and Other Poems*, p. 6.

39. *The Testament of an Empire-Builder*, p. 63.

40. *The Testament of a Prime Minister*, p. 59.

41. *Holiday and Other Poems*, p. 144.

42. *Outlook* (February 11, 1905), 193–94.

43. *The Testament of John Davidson*, p. 46.

## Chapter Seven

1. *Fleet Street and Other Poems*, p. 45.

2. "Hors-D'Oeuvre," *Westminster Gazette* (August 25, 1902), 2.

3. Townsend, pp. 489–96.

4. Grant Richards, *Housman, 1897–1936* (New York, 1942), p. 74. Townsend quotes the same passage on p. 392.

5. A. S. Mories, "The Religious Significance of John Davidson," *Westminster Review*, 180 (July, 1913), 82.

6. This is a paraphrase of Filson Young, "The New Poetry," *Fortnightly Review*, 91 (January 1, 1909), 138.

# Selected Bibliography

PRIMARY SOURCES

1. A Chronological List of Davidson's Published Books

*The North Wall.* Glasgow: Wilson and McCormick, 1885.

*Diabolus Amans: A Dramatic Poem.* Glasgow: Wilson and McCormick, 1885 (Anonymous).

*Bruce: A Drama in Five Acts.* Glasgow and London: Wilson and Mc-Cormick, 1886.

*Smith: A Tragedy.* Glasgow: F. W. Wilson and Brother, 1888.

*Plays.* Greenock: John Davidson (privately printed), 1889. (Includes *An Unhistorical Pastoral,* w. 1877; *A Romantic Farce,* w. 1878; and *Scaramouch in Naxos,* w. 1888. Reissued as *Scaramouch in Naxos: A Pantomime and Other Plays.* London: T. Fisher Unwin, 1890.)

*Perfervid: The Career of Ninian Jamieson.* London: Ward and Downey, 1890.

*The Great Men* and *A Practical Novelist.* London: Ward and Downey, 1891 (*A Practical Novelist* is a reissue of *The North Wall*).

*In a Music-Hall and Other Poems.* London: Ward and Downey, 1891.

*Persian Letters.* 2 vols. London: Privately Printed, 1892 (a translation of Montesquieu).

*Laura Ruthven's Widowhood.* 3 vols. London: Lawrence and Bullen, 1892 (with C. J. Wills).

*Fleet Street Eclogues.* London: Elkin Mathews and John Lane, 1893.

*Sentences and Paragraphs.* London: Lawrence and Bullen, 1893.

*A Random Itinerary.* London: Elkin Mathews and John Lane and Boston: Copeland and Day, 1894.

*Ballads and Songs.* London: John Lane and Boston: Copeland and Day, 1894.

*Baptist Lake.* London: Ward and Downey, 1894.

*Plays.* London: Elkin Mathews and John Lane and Chicago: Stone and Kimball, 1894. (Includes *An Unhistorical Pastoral, A Romantic Farce, Bruce: A Chronicle Play, Smith: A Tragic Farce,* and *Scaramouch in Naxos: A Pantomime.*)

*A Full and True Account of the Wonderful Mission of Earl Lavender.* London: Ward and Downey, 1895.

*St. George's Day: A Fleet Street Eclogue.* New York: John Lane, 1895.

*A Second Series of Fleet Street Eclogues.* London: John Lane and New York: Dodd, Mead and Co., 1895.

*For the Crown: A Romantic Play.* London: Nassau Press, 1896 (a translation and adaptation of François Coppée's *Pour la Couronne*).

*Miss Armstrong's and Other Circumstances.* London: Methuen and Co., 1896.

*The Pilgrimage of Strongsoul and Other Stories.* London: Ward and Downey, 1896.

*New Ballads.* London and New York: John Lane, 1897.

*Godfrida: A Play in Four Acts.* New York and London: John Lane, 1898.

*The Last Ballad and Other Poems.* London and New York: John Lane, 1899.

*Self's the Man: A Tragi-Comedy.* London: Grant Richards, 1901.

*The Testament of a Vivisector.* London: Grant Richards, 1901.

*The Testament of a Man Forbid.* London: Grant Richards, 1901.

*The Testament of an Empire-Builder.* London: Grant Richards, 1902.

*The Knight of the Maypole: A Comedy in Four Acts.* London: Grant Richards, 1903.

*A Rosary.* London: Grant Richards, 1903.

*A Queen's Romance: A Version of Victor Hugo's "Ruy Blas."* London: Grant Richards, 1904.

*The Testament of a Prime Minister.* London: Grant Richards, 1904.

*Selected Poems.* London and New York: John Lane, 1904.

*The Theatrocrat: A Tragic Play of Church and Stage.* London: Grant Richards, 1905.

*The Ballad of a Nun.* London and New York: John Lane, 1905.

*Holiday and Other Poems, with a Note on Poetry.* London: Grant Richards, 1906.

*The Triumph of Mammon.* London: Grant Richards, 1907.

*Mammon and His Message.* London: Grant Richards, 1908.

*The Testament of John Davidson.* London: Grant Richards, 1908.

*Fleet Street and Other Poems.* London: Grant Richards, 1909.

2. A Chronological List of Editions and Selections of Davidson's Works, Published Since His Death

*The Man Forbid and Other Essays.* With an introduction by Edward J. O'Brien. Boston: Ball Publishing Co., 1910.

*Poems by John Davidson.* Introduction by R. M. Wenley. New York: Boni and Liveright, 1924 (Modern Library Edition).

Selected Bibliography

*John Davidson.* Ed. Edward Thompson. London: Ernest Benn, 1925
(The Augustan Books of Modern Poetry).
*Poems and Ballads by John Davidson.* Ed. Robert Duncan Macleod.
London: Unicorn Press, 1959.
*John Davidson: A Selection of His Poems.* Ed. Maurice Lindsay, preface
by T. S. Eliot, with an essay by Hugh McDairmid. London:
Hutchinson, 1961.

3. A List of Bibliographies of Davidson's Writings

*Cambridge Bibliography of English Literature,* vol. 3, p. 337.
LESTER, JOHN A., JR. "John Davidson: A Grub Street Bibliography,"
*Secretary's News Sheet,* The Bibliographical Society of the Uni-
versity of Virginia, September, 1958. See annotation in next
section.
MONCRIEFF, C. K. SCOTT. "John Davidson," *London Mercury,* IV (July,
1921), 299–300.
STONEHILL, C. A., and H. W. *Bibliographies of Modern Authors.* Sec-
ond Series. London, 1925.
TOWNSEND, J. B. "The Quest for John Davidson," *Princeton University
Library Chronicle,* XIII (1952), 123–42.
WENLEY, R. M. "Bibliographical Note." *Poems by John Davidson*
New York: Boni and Liveright, 1924 (Modern Library Edition),
pp. 137–40.

SECONDARY SOURCES

LESTER, JOHN A., JR. "Friedrich Nietzsche and John Davidson: A Study
of Influence," *Journal of the History of Ideas,* XVIII (June, 1957),
411–29. This article answers the question of the extent of Nietzsche's influence on Davidson as fully as it can be answered. It
supersedes any prior study of this question and will remain the
standard source on this relationship.
———. "John Davidson, a Grub Street Bibliography," *Secretary's News
Sheet,* The Bibliographical Society of the University of Virginia,
September, 1958. This very useful bibliography lists over three
hundred items published by Davidson in newspapers and periodicals from 1889 to 1909. It also indicates if they were reprinted and
where. A knowledge of these writings is indispensable in getting a
full view of Davidson's literary and artistic activity during the last
twenty years of his life. Many of his personal viewpoints are expressed in the periodical writings.
TOWNSEND, J. BENJAMIN. *John Davidson: Poet of Armageddon.* New
Haven: Yale University Press, 1961. While many books about English poetry and poets of the late nineteenth and early twentieth

centuries discuss Davidson, all of them have been superseded by Townsend's book which is a thorough critical biography. The biography is well done and as full as it can be at this time; the critical discussion of the poetry and plays is excellent. However, little is said about Davidson's prose fiction.

WENLEY, R. M. "Introduction." *Poems by John Davidson*. New York: Boni and Liveright, 1924 (Modern Library Edition). This twenty-eight-page essay by Wenley is the best brief treatment of Davidson I know of. Wenley covers the biographical facts, but his essay is valuable chiefly because he sees Davidson as the product of a heritage of extreme Protestantism, and I believe no other single factor is so central to understanding Davidson's development.

# Index

*Index*